Analytics in a Business Context

Michael O'Neil

with contributions by members of the
Vision to Value (V2V) Best Practice Community

Foreword by Frank Vella, Chief Executive Officer,
Information Builders

ISBN: 978-0-9938652-7-5 (InsightaaS Press)

Dedication

We live in a time where creation is a collaborative activity. When I was growing up, I remember teachers insisting that each student "do your own work." I don't believe this admonition was ever directed at my daughter, though; students today, including those who pass through my University of Toronto School of Continuing Studies course on Cloud Systems in Practice, are expected to work together to produce deliverables that are improved by each group member's insights and abilities.

No one has benefitted more from this pro-teamwork environment than me. I am incredibly fortunate to collaborate with a community of talented individuals who are committed to co-creating a collective understanding that none of us would be able to author individually. Over the past year, the Vision to Value (V2V) best practice community has been defined by the contributions of dozens of professionals who have seized the opportunity to add their insights to a communal effort to advance the use of facts to shape practices and decisions.

These contributions have created a whole that is truly reflective of the sum of its brilliant parts. I – and all who benefit from the guidance contained in these pages – owe the contributors to this book a debt of gratitude. The community in turn has been shaped by Mary Allen, who has given InsightaaS its sense of place and purpose, and by Stephen Symonds, who has managed each community activity.

V2V would not exist without the vision and support of Information Builders. I'd like to thank Caterina Didio-Duggan for her unwavering faith in V2V; she and her colleagues have matched the curiosity of the V2V community with their own, nurturing a dialog on analytics that now radiates across Canada, and beyond.

Contents

Dedication 3

Foreword: Moving beyond the analytics crossroads...........................9

    The value of being proactive 13

    We are...where?..15

    Survival – and success...17

Developing the Analytics Business Case 19

    The rationale for investing in development of an analytics business case 21

        Building the analytics business case: process drivers..................22

        Building the analytics business case: target outcomes 23

        Building alignment in the analytics business case development process 25

    Business objectives associated with developing the analytics business case 28

        Internal: data management..28

        Internal: outcome focused 30

        'The bridge': connecting internal and external objectives..........31

        External: outcome focused 32

        Summary..33

    Best practices in developing the analytics business case...............33

    Metrics and milestones 37

Problem Solving: The Right Data for the Right Question 41

    Identifying the challenge(s) 43

Challenge 1: the right question, or the right data? 44

Correcting for 'wrong' questions..47

   Aligning questions with evidence limits 48

'The right data': Quality and completeness.................................52

   Two paths to clarity 53

Best practice advice 57

   Final thoughts: applying metrics...61

Monetizing Data: Identifying and Capturing the ROI on Analytics......63

Identifying the sources of data value 65

   Use of data to inform immediate/direct/tactical actions 66

   Use of data to improve processes, control costs, and/or drive efficiency and productivity 67

   Use of data to inform corporate/strategic decisions 70

   Direct data monetization 73

Data monetization best practices...75

   Data monetization: a process view..78

Metrics used to evaluate data monetization.................................81

Establishing Analytics Within the Organization.............................85

Factors in establishing demand for analytics within the organization 87

   Culture 87

   Process evolution...89

   Demonstrable success 90

   Information utility...91

Cautions/potential barriers to creating demand for analytics within an organization 92

The impetus for establishing analytics: top-down or department-out? 95

Top-down 95

Department-out 96

The best of both worlds? 96

Key inputs to the process of establishing analytics within the organization 98

Skills and training 99

Policies 100

Data quality 101

Relevance 101

Solution licensing 102

The evolution of analytics within the organization 104

Getting the ball rolling 104

Timing 105

Integrating analytics within broader corporate policy structures 105

The path forward 109

Cautions 110

Outlook 111

Contributing Experts 113

Contributors to this document 115

Contributors to V2V Meetups...126

Lead analyst 127

Founding member organizations..128

About Information Builders 128

About InsightaaS 128

Foreword: Moving beyond the analytics crossroads
Frank Vella, CEO, Information Builders

Business analytics is at a crucial point – a crossroads. On one hand, everywhere you look in the economy you see growing belief in the value of data. When I meet with customers – of all sizes, in all industries, around the world – I'm constantly told that "data is the new oil." Even the oil companies themselves believe that! A strategist at Royal Dutch Shell wrapped a major project with the conclusion that the company needed to move past just understanding how to drill for oil effectively. In today's market, he said that Shell needs to capitalize on its insights – its information on drilling, information on markets and information on trends – because Shell's historical position as a major corporation and its vast physical assets no longer provide the competitive advantage they once did.

At the same time, we have a persistent problem with the use of data. Even though data is known to have value, the adoption of business intelligence (BI) or analytics within organizations has not grown all that much; within organizations that have deployed analytics systems, the proportion of employees who use BI tools hovers around 30%.

How do organizations make the leap from understanding that their data is valuable to unlocking the value in that data? There are several different initiatives that contribute to driving greater returns from analytics, including the development of data trust, building effective support for data users and creating a clear vision of how analytics will change – and benefit – your organization.

Let's start with data trust. In many organizations, there will be departments that use a set of Excel spreadsheets to analyze a focused set of data and make decisions. That's a reasonable approach to arriving at a quick answer to a quick question but it doesn't scale. If you start making decisions that are big enough to impact the company, you need to be certain that you have data from all relevant corporate sources and a spreadsheet can't support that. In today's enterprise, data can be housed in more than 100 different databases, hosted in the cloud, on mainframes and everywhere in between. If you have legacy systems, if you have had siloed operations or have made an acquisition – you will find that you have data in a wide range of formats and locations. Typically, you'll discover that no one has managed to assemble, synthesize and clean all of these disparate data sets, and unless you establish data integrity, you can't really trust your analytics. Users may begin by looking for an answer but quickly discover that they need data governance before they get there.

That is a really frustrating scenario for most users. Nobody wants to spend three quarters of their time assembling and checking data and have only a few hours left for analysis and decision making. They don't want to worry about where to *get* data; they want ready access to relevant, trusted data. When they have that, they can be more creative in applying data to business decisions and contribute to corporate momentum toward greater use of analytics systems.

The second issue, support for data users, is one that we have been really focused on. The idea that data offers value leads to a belief that data should be everywhere, in every user's hands. But not every user can look at a table or a chart and immediately understand why it's important, what it means and what actions they should take as a result. And if they can't intuitively translate data into understanding, they must be supported with tools that help them to extract meaning from information.

These tools don't need to be complex; in fact, simple tools work best in many situations. For example, we have found that adding a narrative description of what's on a chart helps to illuminate important details. A narrative box might tell the reader something like, "This chart contains a year-over-year comparison of sales results: here are the highlights, this is the average, these are the regions that did the best, these are the lowlights, these units are meaningfully below the norm." That's not complicated but it helps people to identify the areas that they will want to understand better, the situations where they need to drill down.

There are a number of tools that help frame data so it can be used to convey meaning and support conversations or actions. One that's getting a lot of attention today is infographics. We are helping companies to assemble multiple data points into a graphical, storyboard format that is automatically customized for every recipient – every staff member who wants to understand their health plan usage patterns, every customer who wants to visualize the performance of their investment portfolio over time. That kind of tool makes data more accessible: it leads to an explosion of data use as information becomes part of every communication, every process, every decision that is made.

Organizations that can develop an effective analytics business case and deliver support for users who are looking to find the right data to answer the right questions are mature relative to the business community as a whole. Those who really optimize returns on data are able to add a third element: a clear vision of how data will benefit their operations and how to establish demand for data throughout the organization.

Each of these objectives are complicated but in different ways. With data value, one of the core requirements is defining the form that benefits will take and establishing the processes and metrics needed to achieve appropriate goals. When you use the phrase "data monetization," executives are apt to envision that somehow data is crunched, and a dollar bill falls out of the end of the process. That's not necessarily the case, though often, the greatest benefits are gained when manual processes are automated and increased productivity is the immediate return.

For example, there is a great deal of consolidation occurring in the US healthcare sector, with hospitals, clinics and insurers looking to establish greater efficiency. But without sound data processes, there's a greater risk of missing information that can impact treatment or billing. Is the Frank Vella who is checking into the hospital the same Frank Vella who visited a clinic three months ago, or the same F Vella who took an ambulance to a different hospital last fall?

It's possible to assign teams of people to answer these questions – or it's possible to use analytics to automate responses to the majority of them, and to have a much smaller team address the 7% that can't be resolved by the algorithms. Building an analytics-based approach that delivers faster mediation for most questions (improving accuracy, reducing fraud and enhancing customer relationships) and requires a smaller team to resolve the remaining questions is an example of data monetization.

The second objective, establishing demand for analytics through the organization is really a question of culture. Businesses succeed in this when they are able to create an environment where data continuously and positively impacts interactions between colleagues, or between staff and customers or staff and suppliers. In this scenario, references to data aren't an event, they are simply the way of life within the organization. As a supplier, we will see this reflected in the utilization of BI tools – when usage levels get to 60-70% of employees, we know that the organization has built the foundation needed to support a data-driven culture: it has the right aggregation of data, it has high levels of data integrity, it has encouraged employee access and the staff is able to use the system creatively to address their priorities. And we see this in the operational results of these businesses too: they are efficient, they are attractive to customers and employees, and they deliver good returns to their shareholders.

The value of being proactive
This description of how trusted data, support for data users and a clear vision for driving benefit and culture combine to create business value would seem to make a compelling case for launching a systematic analytics strategy within every enterprise – and naturally, I agree that this would be a sound strategy! In reality though, many organizations don't take proactive steps towards developing effective, enterprise-wide analytics capabilities. Frequently, the key driver is a crisis that lands on the desk of the CEO or the CFO who says, "I can't continue without a clear understanding of what's happening in the business any longer. We need to bring all the data together and we need to have data we can trust that we can make decision on."

It might be the case that the company has misread its market and is losing sales to competitors. Or the crisis might be external – a tornado that knocks out corporate infrastructure, forcing a rebuild but also creating an opportunity for new management and delivery approaches. Crises create a difficult starting point since there is pressure to make decisions quickly, while a considered, enterprise BI strategy focuses on making the best decisions, not the fastest ones. It takes a strong executive team to get beyond the 'tyranny of the immediate' and establish a solid basis for insight, but these are the firms that get past crises and regain market momentum.

Where the analytics strategy is proactive, it's often driven by one of two types of developments. Sometimes, recognition of the need for a data strategy falls out of a machine learning (ML) or artificial intelligence (AI) deployment, because the scale of these systems demands data integrity. An individual can make a finite number of decisions in a day; a team of many individuals can increase this number but the overall scope is still limited to how fast individuals or groups can move. When you assign those decisions to machines though, it's possible to accelerate decision processes by hundreds or thousands of times. As a result, the potential impact of data or logic errors on the decision-making process is also hundreds or thousands of times greater than would be the case if individuals, who move relatively slowly and often rely on experience or even instinct in addition to data, make each decision. The adoption path for ML or AI needs to include a structured approach to analyzing, integrating and maintaining data.

The other relatively common proactive driver is the deployment of connected, automated systems. For example, an organization might decide to automate its production and distribution operations. It could deploy systems that take sales data and based on that, make decisions on how to set up a manufacturing line, systems that assign products to a trailer or a truck, and systems that monitor equipment efficiency, maintenance and replacement needs. Within a traditional business, these are typically independent tasks, but each produces data that can be used to improve results in other processes, and which can be aggregated to deliver a cohesive view of the operation. This is almost the inverse of the crisis scenario, but it lands at the same spot: a need to establish a framework and some central oversight to execute on a corporate-wide BI strategy.

We are...where?

Viewed from a corporate management perspective, the keys to analytics success – data trust, support for data users and a vision of how data will benefit and change the organization – converge on the need for an analytics roadmap. Businesses that are looking to establish an evidence-based culture, to ensure that decisions are informed by facts and forward-looking insight, need reliable data to move ahead. Their staff needs to trust in the data so that they can trust in the decisions that result from use of the data. Organizations need to understand how they are going to connect systems and users together so that they can extend insights from conference rooms into the hands of users everywhere in the organization. And they need to act on those insights – they need to capture the value locked in their corporate information. They need to refine this 'new oil' into the fuel that powers their businesses in the knowledge economy.

Creating an analytics roadmap requires understanding and guidance. Organizations that want to define a path forward need to take an approach that covers all of the important foundational steps. And that's why I'm proud that Information Builders has sponsored the research that is included in this book and proud that I've been asked to offer this foreword for it.

As a senior executive, I know that the journey of a thousand miles doesn't begin with a single step. It begins with a vision crystalized in a sound business plan. And from an analytics perspective, that plan needs to reflect a commitment to position data at the core of the business; it needs to consider people, processes and technology; it needs to start with a clear view of the current reality but also have objectives that stretch into the future. The plan needs to recognize that data only really matters when it's used, when it informs decisions and connects directly to action. The analytics business plan is not a document that is designed simply to justify a one-off expenditure – it's a blueprint for a process that drives positive change.

Let me give you an example of how this works in practice. One of our customers is a big credit card company. They have designed their employee portal so that every day, when each employee logs in, they see KPIs that have been identified by the CEO and the senior leadership team as the ones that are most important to the overall health and value of the company – metrics like how many new credit cards have been issued, purchase volume trends and other key data points. The portal is designed to show each employee how their department contributes to these goals. If I'm in a department that focuses on merchant activity, I click on that metric and because my permissions allow me a view into that activity. I can drill progressively deeper into the stats around merchant card services and understand how the company is performing in that area. If I'm in a different department – say, card acquisition – I may not be able to drill deeply into merchant services, but I do know that at a corporate level, this is important to the health of my company, and I can get deeper into the key issues that are tied to the work that I'm doing in card acquisition.

Ultimately, data is used to focus employees from all departments on the company's most important strategic objectives and metrics and helps ensure that everyone in the company is working on things that directly align with corporate goals. Broad data dissemination is also a powerful way to stimulate high adoption levels for analytics. If you show employees where the business needs to go and where they are on the path, they will look for ways to contribute to success.

This idea of inclusiveness – of driving greater use of and usefulness of analytics – is really important. In many environments today, IT provides data aggregation and BI for specific internal customers or even external customers, but it isn't focused on delivering tools that support the organization as a whole. And as a result, at the other end of the spectrum, departmental staff are not getting what they want or feel they need from IT. They are buying end-user tools for business analytics and focusing on their individual needs, or their team needs, or their department's needs.

But when IT is focused on a narrow set of requirements and end-users apply their own tools and data to individual needs, a gap is created at the core of the operation. Management can't assemble a consistent view that aggregates departments into divisions, and divisions into the company as a whole. Businesses that benefit the most from BI move past this point: they establish a corporate BI direction, they identify key KPIs, they build trusted data lakes or data warehouses and they develop corporate applications that support individual needs in ways that align with broad objectives. These organizations are positioned for growth in a knowledge-based economy.

Survival – and success
Following all this discussion of other companies' data, let me close with a data point of my own.

Company lifespans are shrinking. A <u>2018 study of the lifespan of US firms on the S&P 500</u> shows a dramatic decline: the average tenure of companies on the index was 33 years in 1964, but this narrowed to 24 years in 2016 and is forecast to shrink by another 50%, to 12 years, by 2027.[1] If the current churn rate continues, half of the S&P will be replaced over the next decade. And as dire as this sounds for large enterprises, it's even worse for <u>smaller businesses, where lifespans</u> are even shorter: nearly half of small businesses exit before their fifth anniversary.[2]

It's pretty clear that technology is an important factor in these diminishing lifespans: barriers to entry into virtually every industry are lower than they ever were before and that's a function of new market entrants capitalizing on technology – lower cost of infrastructure with cloud and greater access to skilled workers who can connect virtually from any location.

But while technology can pose a threat, it's also a solution. Companies that develop fact-based insights improve their positions. The businesses that are bucking the shorter lifecycle trend and thriving over the longer term are capitalizing on the insights that they glean from their data. They are gaining competitive advantage from understanding how to differentiate based on what they know about their customers, about their market and about the opportunities that they can and should develop. And this isn't just true for executives and decision makers. Data is now core to every role in a company. Businesses that are successful in establishing analytics in a business context are poised to succeed today and in tomorrow's marketplace.

---

[1] <u>2018 Corporate Longevity Forecast: Creative Destruction is Accelerating</u>. Innosight
[2] <u>A large share of small businesses are young businesses</u>. JP Morgan Chase

Chapter 1.

Developing the Analytics Business Case

Contributing community experts: Mary Allen, InsightaaS; May Chang, formerly of Markham Stouffville Hospital; Caterina Didio-Dugan, Information Builders; Francis Jeanson, Datadex; Brian Joynt, Information Builders; Dean McKeown, Queen's School of Business; Michael Proulx, Pride Conflict Management; Purushoth Ramu, LexisNexis; Don Sheppard, ConCon Management Services; Michael Shin, Ontario Government; Roman Zubarev, 29signals Consulting

Initial publication date: January 2018

Developing the Analytics Business Case

The rationale for investing in development of an analytics business case

"The journey of a thousand miles begins with one step."

"Really, that's not true. Every major journey begins with a plan"

Laozi

Data scientist Randal Olson

It's generally recognized – despite the ancient, oft-cited wisdom of Chinese philosopher Laozi – that a complex endeavour needs to begin with a plan. But as is frequently the case with received wisdom, little attention is paid to the reasons for investing in the plan, and the benefits that it can produce (beyond a general sense of order). Organizations commit to documenting proposed analytics initiatives, but rarely examine the rationale for development of the analytics business case – to the detriment of the plan and the approach that it articulates.

In considering the business case for analytics, the V2V working group launched its investigation by addressing the 'why?' question: why is developing the analytics business case important? The group also reviewed the related context: what is changing – in terms of technology, market opportunity or competitive pressure – that makes business case development important?

Throughout the working group session, focus wavered between two separate, but interconnected issues: the development of the case itself, and the objectives for the process described in the case. This two-threaded approach can introduce complexity into discussions of the rationale for investing in development of an analytics business case, but ultimately, it is beneficial: the plan and the process and outcomes it describes are both important, and need to be linked to ensure that analytics professionals take the most direct and surest path to realization of technology benefits. Organizations that understand the analytics business case objectives optimize their chances of building relevant, comprehensive plans, and of ultimately delivering superior analytics initiative results.

Building the analytics business case: process drivers

What drives companies to view the analytics journey as critical to their success, leads to investment in development of the analytics business case, and what is important to building the structure needed to harvest benefit from data-reliant investigations? The working group identified a range of drivers that are prompting action in Canadian organizations today:

- A desire to identify and quantify the value of data within the organization.
- A need to increase internal readiness for analytics adoption; to begin building a foundation for a culture that will accept data as a core component of operations (in both strategy and execution).
- A commitment to collecting, organizing and analyzing data to identify issues in the business (use of descriptive/diagnostic analytics).
- An appreciation of the need to plot out a path to use of advanced analytics to keep pace with a fast-moving global environment. This can be seen as an extension of the

previous point, where organizations see a need to move beyond basic analytics in order to accelerate or automate tasks.

- A recognition that organizations realize benefits when they are able to turn data into intelligence. An increasingly digitized business environment produces a great deal of data, but that data is only beneficial when organizations develop an approach to aggregating and learning from the expanding range of inputs.

Figure 1-1. Building the analytics case: Process drivers and target outcomes

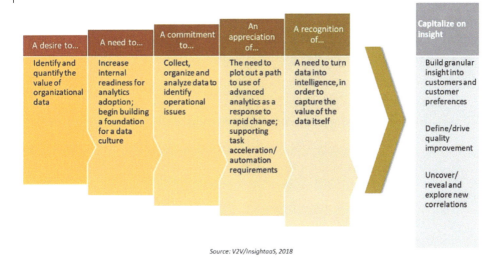

Source: V2V/InsightaaS, 2018

Building the analytics business case: target outcomes

A second set of motivators for analytics business case development, defined as the corporate goals that prompt investment in analytics initiatives, is associated with results rather than process. Based on outcomes, the rationale for investing in an analytics business case is not necessarily linked to the desire to optimize analytics processes, but rather to shape the approach used to deliver on business objectives.

There are many different outcomes that could prompt development of a supportive analytics business case. Three that were highlighted by the working group included:

- *Understanding customers.* Advances in technology (compute and the ability to aggregate large volumes of internal and relevant third-party data) allow companies to understand customers and customer preferences at a very granular level. The analytics business case is tremendously important here: it maps out the process by which companies will identify future customers and products, improve customer relationships and services – necessary competencies in a digital world.
- *Improve quality.* Another example offered by the working group focused on quality improvements. In this case, the analytics business case articulates the ways that data will be collected and used to identify and redress process or product problems, providing benchmark information that motivates individual improvement. The example raised in the discussion centred on the healthcare environment, but the principles could be applied in many different settings.
- *Uncover/reveal and explore new correlations.* This is really a two-part planning issue. The first step is to identify a broad area that would benefit from examination, which creates a business case for aggregation and analysis of internal and relevant external data. The second is to use the results of this analysis to identify opportunities for improvement in the target area. The example used in the working group

discussion concerned environmental/CSR issues – but again, the approach of using analytics to increase the scope of executive/corporate understanding and action is applicable in multiple areas.

Building alignment in the analytics business case development process

There's no single 'right answer' that can determine whether development of an analytics business case should focus on outcomes or on an examination of the process itself; both are important. The key to creating an effective analytics business case is to align each of the key factors – executive objectives, a need/opportunity to capitalize on data, a requirement to impose structure on data-reliant investigations and development of a link between the process and its target outcomes – in a single process. The business case is the

> The business case is the vehicle by which those who are advocates for change describe the possible future and the process by which it will be delivered.

vehicle by which those who are advocates for change describe the possible future and the process by which it will be delivered.

In Figure 1-2. below, alignment is shown as beginning with an understanding of executive objectives. The use of the plural (objectives) is intentional; executives have a wide range of strategic and tactical goals. Analytics projects can launch in response to a single objective or to tackle a discrete, defined set of connected aims; wide-ranging objectives are best addressed through a succession of business cases that target different elements of a central issue. This is an important 'macro' consideration in building alignment in the analytics business case development process: it isn't necessary (nor even desirable) to try to solve all aspects of a complex business problem with a single overarching project; it is much better to work iteratively through the planning and delivery process, delivering substantive change through a series of targeted and measurable initiatives.

The next stages shown in the Figure involve data and process. What is the best way to capitalize on internal (and relevant/complementary external) data, to deliver insight that is applicable to the target executive objective(s)? And what is the best way to structure the analytics initiative to use this data to deliver the insights needed for success?

The final stage is a major issue in many organizations: what is the key to establishing the importance of data in the decision-making process? Many companies lack a 'data culture' that treats analytics as an essential element in determining direction; in many contexts, data is used to justify opinions rather than to shed new light on important issues. The working group noted repeatedly that part of the business case process involves 'earning trust' by setting attainable goals and demonstrating success.

Figure 1-2. Building alignment in the analytics business case development process

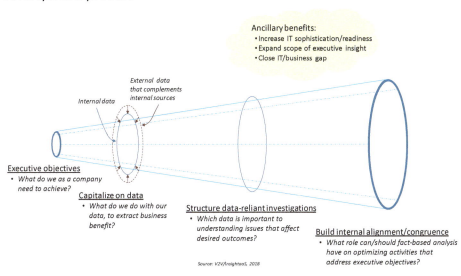

Outside of the initiative 'telescope' – but still important to the business case assembly process – are a set of ancillary benefits, which should be viewed as benefits of effective analytics business plan development. These include:

- Expanding the scope of executive insight by delivering new insights, which in turn increases the range of operational options available to the organization.
- Increasing IT sophistication/readiness by bringing IT into projects that have clear, tangible business benefit, and aligning IT activities with business requirements.
- Closing the IT/business gap by engaging stakeholders from both areas in definition of a common plan.

These ancillary benefits don't need to be called out within the plan, but they should be discussed as goals associated with, and realized through the planning process.

Business objectives associated with developing the analytics business case

The second major question tackled by the working group was "What is the business objective associated with developing the analytics business case? If we're successful, what will change in the organization?"

Responses to this question can be grouped into four categories: *internal data management, internal outcomes, building the 'bridge' between internal and external outcomes,* and *external outcomes.* Key issues raised under each of these headings, and examples of the changes that they drive, are detailed below.

Internal: data management

Securing required resources. If a firm's objective is to make better use of data, it's important to understand whether there is sufficient expertise in house to work with data and produce targeted results, or whether the organization will need to hire additional resources or engage external suppliers. If internal capabilities are an issue, the business case should be clear on the preferred strategy for obtaining necessary skills or bandwidth.

Establish effective governance. Over time and across varying objectives, it is inevitable that some data will be required by multiple projects, and that some of the required data will be sensitive or subject to regulatory control or audit. Organizations need to ensure that sensitive data is managed in accordance with compliance requirements, and at the same time, need to be sure that data used in every initiative is consistent (with data used in other investigations) and complete (so that decisions are based on best

-available evidence). Data governance standards should be incorporated within each analytics business case, and should reflect policies that span all use cases: the organization should have standards (or defined stages) for data integration and management to ensure that outcomes (for example, decisions on new product developments or customer management approaches) are based on complete and reliable insights, while also assuring management that use of the data is consistent with applicable regulatory and best practice standards. Over time, this adherence to sound governance standards will build trust in corporate data, and confidence in decisions based on that data.

> When everybody knows what data they have, where it is, that it's accessible, that it's compliant…it tremendously improves operational efficiency. Tasks that took months and teams take hours and 1-2 people…

Create one version of the truth. Creation of a single standard for evidence used in analytics initiatives may be outside the scope of a business case targeted at a discrete outcome – but it should be an objective within each analytics business case. It isn't possible to identify – or at least, to compare – areas that require executive attention if the data used in the comparisons (across departments, time or other dimensions) is inconsistent. Each analytics business case should include a plan for ensuring that data is consistent and coherent.

Internal: outcome focused

Optimize quality. Not every analytics initiative is focused on quality, but the ability to assess quality is dependent on credible, meaningful data that is granular enough to show gaps between different actions or between an action and its target outcome. There may be no requirement to include quality improvements within an analytics case – but in some situations, there may be an ability to identify ways that analytics outcomes could contribute to a clearer understanding of current and achievable quality levels.

Improve productivity. Part of the function of the analytics group within an organization should be to establish an "information supply chain" that captures and manages data to deliver best possible outcomes with the greatest amount of automation and repeatability. Firms that define this supply chain – again, both at a corporate level and within the context of a specific business case – should be able to enhance the productivity of analytics resources and the business users/units that they serve.

Drive process efficiencies. Aligning data with strategic decisions and tactical approaches allows for establishment of a consistent, top-to-bottom vision of the actions that can and should be taken at all levels of the organization. This fact-based insight into current vs. desired states can help drive (and improve connections between) process efficiencies across multiple individuals, processes and departments.

Figure 1-3. Business objectives driving analytics business case development

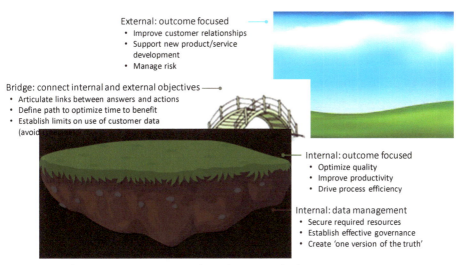

External: outcome focused
- Improve customer relationships
- Support new product/service development
- Manage risk

Bridge: connect internal and external objectives
- Articulate links between answers and actions
- Define path to optimize time to benefit
- Establish limits on use of customer data (avoid

Internal: outcome focused
- Optimize quality
- Improve productivity
- Drive process efficiency

Internal: data management
- Secure required resources
- Establish effective governance
- Create 'one version of the truth'

'The bridge': connecting internal and external objectives

Articulate the links between answers and actions. This is a core requirement of the analytics business case: what answers can be extracted from available data, and how do these answers impact the decisions that management will take in directing operations? This process perspective should be explicit in the analytics business case.

Define the path to optimize time to benefit. An analytics business case should clearly articulate the path that optimizes time to benefit – the process that most quickly and predictably leads from answer to action.

Establish limits on use of customer data. Notwithstanding every other objective highlighted in this section, use of data to personalize responses or offerings can be very unsettling for the customer. Organizations will need to establish corporate guidelines that reduce the 'creepiness factor' in data-rich customer interactions, and reflect these guidelines in individual business cases.

External: outcome focused

Customer intimacy – and reduced churn. Data is used to support a rich, multi-layered approach to customer, and will increasingly be used to define the best possible approaches to customer interactions. As noted above, it's important to avoid being 'creepy' in customer communications. It is also important, though, to use data to identify actions that are wanted or needed. Firms that fail to do this will lose share and relevance; those that do it well can reduce churn and improve customer loyalty. These outcomes help to justify investments in analytics initiatives.

Support new product/service development. Not all analytics initiatives are designed to directly support analysis leading to creation of new products/services, but many of those with the greatest financial impact are. Even those initiatives that have different primary objectives need, at some point, to demonstrate how and why they contribute to the success of the organization. Professionals preparing analytics business cases should be sure to articulate the ways that an initiative leads to refinement or development of the goods or services that the organization uses to establish its value to its clients.

Manage risk. Risk management is more focused on threat than opportunity. However, as an important part of every executive's agenda, risk management resonates with senior management as a reason to invest in initiatives and competencies. There are many ways that analytics helps organizations manage risk (the establishment of a single version of the truth, for example). Analytics professionals should articulate links between their initiatives and corporate risk management wherever the impact is clear and compelling.

Summary

It's evident that the analytics business case can address many different and compelling objectives, triggering change in internal processes and/or external customer engagements. Analytics professionals who are cognizant of these objectives and outcomes are well-positioned to develop and deliver business cases that are clearly aligned with needs and opportunities within the organization.

Best practices in developing the analytics business case

Identifying best practices that should be used in preparing the analytics business case occupied the bulk of the working group's attention. Out of a spirited discussion, the group defined five principles that professionals can use to enhance their own analytics business case development.

1. Each initiative begins by identifying the desired outcome. This is clear in the 'telescope' graphic, which positions executive objectives as the starting point for analytics initiatives. The point was reinforced by the working group: one member noted that most corporate activities have the goal of "make money, save money...[or sometimes], drive cultural change." Additional guidance on this point included the need to be conservative in financial estimates embedded in analytics business cases, especially with respect to impact on future revenue – the group member advised predicating case rationales on 35% of forecasted revenue, in order to focus discussion on process and outcomes rather than on the forecasts themselves.

2. Start with the 'low hanging fruit'. This advice is applied in many contexts, and is useful here as well: the best way to build corporate confidence in a new technology or approach is to quickly deliver tangible benefits, and the best way to achieve *this* (in the words of a working group member) is to "take advantage of simple tasks that can yield substantial gains." A second and related objective is to develop a pattern of success through collaboration; engaging both "information users and information managers" – business and IT professionals – in projects that have limited duration and evident payback, and then recognizing the contributions made by both groups, helps to develop trust and connections that will be valuable in supporting complex future initiatives.

3. Align outcomes with metrics. One expert member of the working group described a framework that spans "problem, approach, outcome and metric." This construct helps ensure that the analytics business case moves predictably from the executive objectives ("problem(s)") to the analytics activity (approach) to the objective ("outcome"), and that it explicitly embeds metrics that can be used to establish the success of the initiative – versus prior state, goals, or both.

4. Engage stakeholders with an interest in the problem or outcome. Most corporate investments are cost justified by comparing the cost of a project to the value of a specific target outcome. This is entirely appropriate in areas where benefits are specific to a discrete process – as they would be, for example, with an investment aimed at ironing out a kink in healthcare claims management procedures – or tied to an individual user or user group, as would be the case if an business acquired a PC, productivity software or even a task-

specific application like a benefits administration package. With analytics, though, it is often the case that a problem or outcome has impact in multiple areas of the organization. Professionals responsible for the development of an analytics business case are urged to identify these adjacent stakeholder groups, and to describe the institutional benefit that will be derived from the analytics initiative. This may not directly affect the core financial evaluation of a project, but identifying and connecting with management in adjacent areas can help amplify both support for an initiative and awareness of its contribution to organizational success.

5. The fifth category of advice pertains to tying individual analytics initiatives (and their business cases) to broader corporate benefits. Analytics experience creates institutional understanding of the ways that analytics projects create both specific and institutional benefit, and of how to handle issues that arise during the delivery process. The guidance on the left side of Figure 1-4. applies to the process of managing specific projects (experiment, learn, optimize), but references as well corporate knowledge that is gained through repeated applications of this process. The guidance on the right – "don't 'boil the ocean' – but don't miss the bigger vision" is intended to describe the relationship between individual projects and overarching corporate objectives. No one project should be scoped so broadly that it will exhaust management patience and support before it is completed, but each project should be designed to build on outcomes and lessons learned from previous initiatives, through processes, deliverables and data treatments that can benefit future analytics endeavours.

This final point led to a working group discussion that surfaces in many analytics conversations: what is the ideal role for 'shared resources' (a formal centre of competency or an informal group of analytics professionals) who support the analytics activities of multiple corporate groups? If the key objective in many analytics initiatives is to get past the limitations imposed by "you don't know what you don't know," a multi-disciplinary team comprised of individuals with different types of skills can contribute perspective and creativity that benefits a wide range of potential engagements, in addition to the skills needed to deliver successfully and the broader understanding needed to impose data governance and develop institutional understanding of best/proven practices. However, this team can sometimes become a barrier to effective use of data. One working group member noted that "you are successful (in building a culture that values analytics) when people ask 'can I go next?'" This kind of impetus towards analytics needs to build within the operating units; a central project team prompting business users to be proactive in their data use isn't helpful to building broad interest and buy-in.

Figure 1-4. Best practices in developing the analytics business case

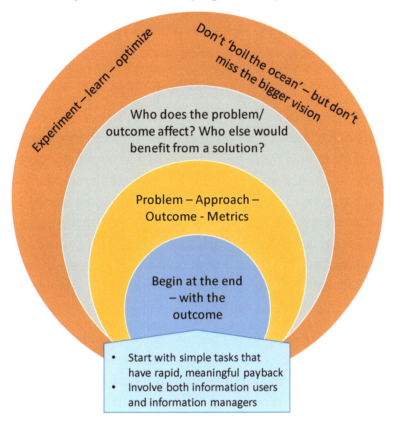

Metrics and milestones

Each Best Practice community managed by InsightaaS[3] ends its investigation of a topic by identifying metrics and milestones that can be used to calibrate the journey towards more effective use of advanced technologies.

---

[3] In addition to V2V, InsightaaS manages the Toronto Cloud Business Coalition, DC Foresight, Transformative Technologies in Canada, IoT Coalition Canada and Canadian Analytics Business Coalition.

Responses from the V2V working group reflected the diverse backgrounds of its members. Different measurements and processes apply in different contexts, and issues that are critical in one industry setting may not apply, or may be understood differently in another.

Observations offered during the working group session included:

Context trumps statistics. One member with a marketing role stated that "You need to develop a combination of numbers and an understanding of how these numbers related to target objectives. In the real world, there may not be a one-to-one relationship between activity and outcome; the analytics plan needs to acknowledge and address complexity." Another member chimed in with the observation that "quantitative analysis is pretty simple; qualitative is more complex," adding to the notion that simple correlations are less important than an appropriately-nuanced understanding of what the statistics mean in context.

Processes need to map to target outcomes. One member with a science background described the process framework as "start with the hypothesis," and structure metrics to support evaluation of sensitivity and impact assessment. The key milestone is arriving at a point where it is possible to do 'what if' analysis using constructed metrics to identify the impact of factors that have effect on a target outcome or situation (for example, the effect of specific factors on behaviour). A second member expanded on this idea, noting that quantifiable outcomes may be more useful for building cohesion across groups (by presenting a shared view of a process, situation, outcome, etc.) than for drilling down into specific success factors.

"Compared to what?" One issue that arose in the metrics and milestones discussion – which isn't consistently raised in corporate

environments – is the basis for measurement. Is analytics success evaluated by comparing a new current state (shaped or informed by analytics) with the previous state? Or is analytics success evaluated against plan? The former would seem to be more germane to an organization, as it evaluates the value of the analytics initiative, but it requires baseline benchmarking that may only exist if it is captured and embedded within the analytics business case; the latter evaluates the success of the case and the accuracy of the planning. Another member noted that the metrics must "always go back to strategy. What metrics are important to gauging progress" at a corporate level, and not simply within a business silo. A third member, agreeing vigorously, pointed to the need to describe milestones in the context of "holistic organizational transformation," adding that "any framework is helpful in navigating from strategy to processes and roles!"

In the end, there is no single set of metrics that serve as a universal measuring stick for analytics success. Each business case should document its own expectations – for change in a specific area, or for cross-functional or corporate-wide impact – and measure achievement against these goals, and improvement over the prior state. By documenting expectations and impediments to change, the process by which data will be applied to drive that change, the outcomes that will result from improved processes and the measures that reflect the magnitude of improvement, the analytics business case becomes much more than a means of cost-justifying a specific investment. It becomes a window and a guide to the future state of the organization.

Chapter 2.

Problem Solving: The Right Data for the Right Question

Contributing community experts: Mary Allen, InsightaaS; Andre Chin, CPP; Caterina Didio-Duggan, Information Builders; Pavan Jauhal, City of Toronto; Francis Jeanson, IAMOPEN; Victor Magdic, Concept Flow; Dean McKeown, Queen's School of Business; Jan Naranowicz, Rogers; Mitchell Ogilvie, Information Builders; Kelly Piggott, Information Builders; Michael Proulx, Pride Conflict Management; Dana Saltern, BusinessOne; Glenda Schmidt, ex-OECM; Vlad Skorokhod, eclairesys; Jeffrey Veffer, Jones Lang LaSalle

Initial publication date: March 2018

Problem solving: The right data for the right question

Identifying the challenge(s)

The report is based on the premise that problem solving is a function of obtaining 'the right data' to answer 'the right question'. Inherent in the title statement is the assumption that organizations seeking information are able to

identify appropriate questions and data sets, and to use data science to develop the insights needed to deliver answers needed by the business to make informed decisions; this in turn requires expertise in structuring questions that are both important to the business and answerable with analytics, and depth in finding and using data that is clean, relevant and complete.

In some cases, this process can become circular – the 'right' question is modified to become 'the question that is answerable with available data', which may result in the entire exercise becoming misaligned with the original business problem. In other cases, appropriate questions are answered with results that are skewed by incomplete or 'dirty' data. Organizations that have established mature analytics practices have learned how to balance the analytics aspirations of business leaders with the realities of data and its uses. In the "Problem solving: the right data for the right question" working group research meeting, the V2V community dug into how this process can and should be managed to deliver best results.

Challenge 1: the right question, or the right data?

The research meeting began by asking "which is a greater challenge – getting questions defined such that they can be appropriately addressed by analytics, or assembling a data set that includes all of the data needed to address the question?"

Of 15 participants in the meeting, 12 offered opinions on the core question: three believed that data is the greater challenge, three believed the question is a greater challenge, and six believe that either or both can be the more difficult issue, depending on context: the availability of data from legacy systems, and the maturity of the organization with respect to understanding how to align what one participant flagged as *two* questions – the domain question, which reads on the business problem, and the data science question, which is a translation of the business question into syntax that can be addressed with analytics. This working group member added that "if you have both the right (data science) question and a complete data set, you can give the question to a graduate student" to solve.

The discussion in this part of the meeting focused on what drives the 'right' question or data. Through the conversation, three key elements were identified as important on each side of the balance. As Figure 2-1 shows, key 'right question' issues start with the *domain* – 'what do we need to know about our business in order to deliver better outcomes?' – and expand to include the *data science* question – 'how should this request be structured, to deliver the best and most reliable answer to the business?' The relationship between these two points is important, as the 'problem solving' objective can get lost in the translation. As one working group member observed that "there's a question that the business *wants* to ask, but [the question morphs] because it can't find the data to satisfy the initial request. Question A turns into question A_1 – now the right question isn't being asked any more, and you're working backwards – you stop asking the question that's needed."

A third issue, *value*, was raised in the discussion as well, with one member noting that "enterprises may be swimming in data, but they need to clean, store and manage data. How does the cost relate – what is the value of the data? Are you asking something of the data that will deliver real value" to the business? This pertains broadly to the overall value of an analytics practice within a business, but it should be incorporated into evaluation of specific inquiries as well. Is the value of having the 'right answer' greater than the cost of generating the needed insight?

Figure 2-1. Problem solving: establishing the balance between 'right question' and 'right data'

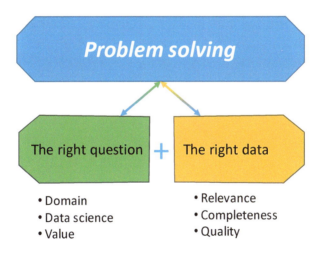

Source: V2V/InsightaaS, 2018

Discussion of the 'right data' side of the equation also focused on three issues. The first was *relevance*: does the data available support development of the insight that the business is seeking? The second, related issue concerned *completeness*: do we have all of the data needed to complete this analysis? This is a common and potentially-pernicious issue – many inquiries are constrained by available data. One member highlighted the fact that "you don't know what you don't know. Ultimately, you want a variety of data sets, and the ability to connect them." Another member stated that "I often start with a very small data set" because that's what the business client has; there's no real question of accessing a 'complete' set of data to answer the question, while a third noted that in "established companies with legacy systems – the business itself [is] siloed, so it was difficult to get accurate (and timely) information."

The last point from the right-hand side of Figure 2-1, *quality*, is bound up in the overall assessment of whether the data is 'right' for evaluation of the business problem. This was a common concern within the working group – one participant stated that "you really do have to have good data" to provide meaningful support for problem solving within the business; another added that "dirty data will return a dirty answer."

At the end of this discussion, participants focused on two words, iteration and maturity. In practice, iteration is important to connecting clean, complete and relevant data to the analysis (though one contributor cautioned that "assembling data sets can lead into correlation mining – I'd rather be looking for the data to answer the right question" than basing questions on data). Maturity, it was generally believed, is the factor that determines whether the question or the data is most likely to be an organization's primary obstacle: "Organizations that are less experienced in terms of analyzing data generally have a harder time with the formation of their questions," while those with more expertise are "usually a lot more accustomed to formulating the questions well, and it's the gathering of the data that will be the bigger challenge for them."

Correcting for 'wrong' questions

Once the groundwork for the 'problem solving' topic was complete, the group delved into each side of the right question/right data issue, starting with examination of the first part of the equation: "Can you offer an example or two from your experience of questions that were 'wrong' – in the sense that they didn't fully address a real business problem – and talk about how you managed this issue, either by reframing the question or by redirecting the (internal or external) client to a different objective?"

While the initial discussion focused on the connection between domain and data science questions, exploration of best paths to the 'right question' quickly expanded to include another issue – tactics vs. strategy. In some cases, what makes a question 'wrong' is mostly a matter of focus. One group member offered this example from a call centre which was trying to optimize their approach to collecting on overdue accounts:

> "One of the questions was 'when are we scheduling our collection agents?' It turned out that *how* we approached the calls was more important than scheduling. What we found was that the scheduling didn't really matter – what was important was the right verbiage and technique."

Another example was raised by a practitioner with experience in the public sector, looking at an organization that was "trying to implement transformation, but taking a project-based approach – everything was tactical." Ultimately, the analytics group needed to persuade senior management of the value of the analytics practice – which in turn, required a more cohesive approach to the discipline of analytics (linking tools like master data management and objectives like predictive analytics) and a better framework for applying these tools to the broader needs of the executives, rather than the specific goals of individual projects.

A third anecdote involved an organization that prioritized specific questions based on the availability of data that would provide credible answers, rather than in terms of the issues that were most pressing for the business. In this case, there were some quick-hit responses, but to questions that weren't particularly meaningful – and the business itself ended up facing a shutdown because the analytics group hadn't determined that it needed to focus on the most critical questions rather than what was readily at hand.

It could be argued that this distinction between focus on tactics vs. business outcomes should be addressed in the original question formulation stage, but it isn't always possible for the analytics professional to redirect the business user's interest in this way. It is possible, though, to infuse analytics discipline with a commitment to iteration – and to use discussion of the answer to a specific question to identify related, and potentially higher value, issues and opportunities.

Aligning questions with evidence limits

Another means of correcting for unfocused or misdirect questions is to elevate business understanding of what can be asked of and answered by the data held by the organization. A participant remembered working with business leaders "to expose them to what the data warehouse contained" and finding that the domain experts "understanding what data was available helped them to ask better questions."

This can be a particularly thorny issue when dealing with survey data, an issue that was raised by several working group members. There are times when the question is not well enough understood by the respondents to represent real answers to a key question, and others where filtering the sample to eliminate non-relevant responses leaves the N values too small for credible analysis.

Other data sources may also fail to fully represent the information needed to make a good decision. For example, referral engines on websites are helpful where they can direct a potential customer to a product that is likely to be of interest – but these engines fail if they *don't* make relevant recommendations, and the recommendations themselves rely on having a rich body of data showing preferences for different types of consumers. If the evidence isn't adequate, the initiative may need to be scaled back until additional data can be added to the analysis.

Other examples of these types of mismatches pertain to the degree of certainty that the business user wants, vs. the type of response that the data will support. One contributor noted that "clients often ask for deterministic, predictive models – but the limits of evidence often will support only a probabilistic model. Business professionals don't like probabilistic – [for example] sales people want to know which deals will close, not the probability of a close!"

In these examples, the basic problem isn't one of focus; instead, the key issue is that the question is too ambitious for the supporting data. In cases of these types, the analytics professional needs to redirect the business person to focus on the benefits that *can* be gained through analytics. One group member identified this as a need to build data maturity, so that business people develop an "understanding of the real value of the data.' The member added that by working collaboratively with business-side clients, the analytics professional may be able to bring attention to "structural areas that are being overlooked that you can see with data…[the result is] not deterministic, but probabilistically, [this type of analysis can] indicate something that you need to fix."

The working group added two observations to this conclusion:

- Involve – meaningfully – stakeholders with different perspectives. In some cases, this will help the analytics professional to re-frame the question to better address business requirements with existing data. In others, it might indicate a flaw in the analytics approach; as one contributor observed, "if the CFO is pushing back [on a question or an answer] you may have to change your problem-solving approach.
    - o This said, as a follow-up point, the group warned against trying to accommodate too may different perspectives. One member called a situation where the call for questions was "opened up to many members of the business community, asking 'what is it that you want to see?' The company ultimately asked too many questions – and unfortunately, that led to a misguided project – and these things do cost money; they need to be managed in such a way that you get best value."

- Make sure that there is a clear path from insight to action. In many cases, if the question needs to be corrected, the best approach to building consensus on a new approach is to get all stakeholders to agree on the business outcomes that they are pursuing, and to use that as a way to open discussion on the question(s) that will best support the activities needed to realize the goal.

Figure 2-2 presents a decision tree-style perspective on the correcting for the wrong question, looking both at issues of focus and of insufficient evidence.

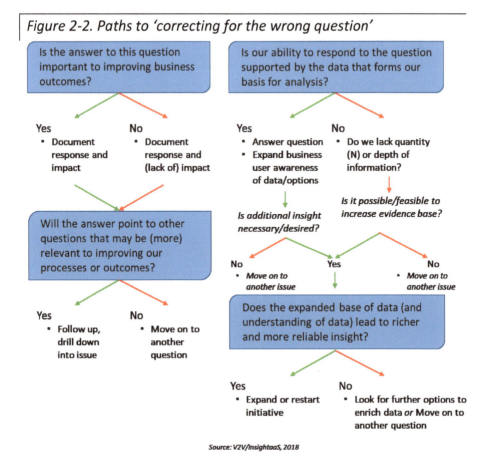

Figure 2-2. Paths to 'correcting for the wrong question'

Source: V2V/InsightaaS, 2018

'The right data': Quality and completeness

The third part of the research discussion focused on the 'right data' side of the equation. It started with a statement – "it's possible to use the wrong data to answer a question – because it's incomplete, or because the data is mismatched from the question, or because it doesn't read on the underlying business objective; similarly, it's possible to use analytics correctly but to arrive at a wrong answer, if the evidence used isn't complete enough to provide accurate guidance" – which led to a question for the group: "how do you make sure that the evidence used in your analytics provides a complete basis for delivering the right answer to the right question?"

The working group, like the analytics community as a whole, found this a difficult question. One member offered that "I don't think knowing if you have the right data is black and white – this is a really gray area."

A group member summarized this initial stage of the discussion by observing that the issue can be framed as "what does it take to convince the audience you're working with?" He then expanded on the first question: "it comes down to – do you have a really sound question in the first place? Does answer map to intuition/experience? Is the science, math and statistics credible?"

Two paths to clarity
Domain understanding
This observation led to a group discussion on the two issues of mapping to domain expert understanding and data science. One response offered by a contributor elicited laughter from the group: "How do I know when I have the right data? When it gives me the answer that I want!"

Beyond the mirth, though, this response was offered in one form or another by many members of the group. When the laughter died down, the working group member added that a domain expert "should have a feel for what the answer should be...if I see that the data and my feeling is totally off, I need to ask more questions, or go to the source and find where the mismatch comes from."

The issue of whether an answer 'makes sense' begs a related question – 'to whom?' Several group members stated that having stakeholders representing multiple points of view is important to establishing the validity of both the data and the answer(s) that it creates.

Before leaving this issue, the working group explored one additional topic: whether using data to support 'an answer' was actually a sufficient outcome to an analytics initiative. One observation along these lines held that "you can't use data to prove a point; all you can do is to use the data to improve the reliability of the answer...you really do need to have some instinct and some knowledge and some contextual understanding that works with the data." A successful data-driven investigation, the member explained, doesn't end with an answer to a question, but rather, an "'aha!' moment."

Figure 2-3. Complementary paths to 'the right data'

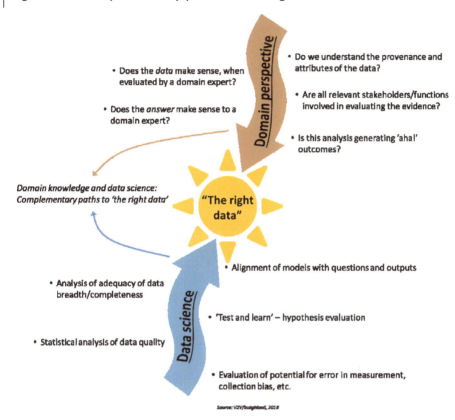

- Does the *data* make sense, when evaluated by a domain expert?
- Does the *answer* make sense to a domain expert?

Domain perspective

- Do we understand the provenance and attributes of the data?
- Are all relevant stakeholders/functions involved in evaluating the evidence?
- Is this analysis generating 'aha!' outcomes?

Domain knowledge and data science: Complementary paths to 'the right data'

"The right data"

- Analysis of adequacy of data breadth/completeness
- Statistical analysis of data quality

Data science

- Alignment of models with questions and outputs
- 'Test and learn' – hypothesis evaluation
- Evaluation of potential for error in measurement, collection bias, etc.

Source: V2V/InsightxS, 2018

Science and quality

As is shown in Figure 2-3, the other path to establishing that the analytics initiative is predicated on 'the right data' is application of data science – building a practitioner-level understanding of data quality (including completeness) and of the 'fit' between models and objectives. One participant observed:

> "A perfect data set would describe the truth in a non-ambiguous manner – but these types of data sets just don't exist in business domains. There is always measurement

error, human error, opinions instead of fact, things like that. This contributes both to data being incomplete because of missing signals, or incorrect because someone made a mistake, or the measurement system didn't work very well, or because our expert is biased towards some type of belief instead of giving us a pure processed view of the data...the point here is that we have to accept [data set flaws] and learn how to deal with it."

In many cases, the group opined, it is difficult to persuade business colleagues that data is not precise, accurate and complete. One member said that business colleagues "think that having MORE data adds greater validity to predictive capabilities, but that's not necessarily the case...just because you have more, it's not improving the predictive quality of what has already been assessed." This focus on aggregating *more* rather than *meaningful* data can have a significant negative effect on decision quality; one working group member recalled a situation where a firm "collected data on every single thing but didn't know what they wanted to find out – too much data, not enough understanding of what the data *should* look like – leads to death by a thousand cuts – we don't know if we have the right data, we don't know if the data is clean, but we start to make decisions based on [the evidence]."

One method of using data science to break through to the right data is an iterative 'test and learn' approach. It can be described in this way: "if you end up with results that you weren't expecting, then you get back into the team (a diverse team of different people from different areas - people who know the data, people who know the business), and start re-evaluating your hypothesis, working through the characteristics of the business problem [and the data], figuring out where you could do better. That's where you can identify bad data, or incompleteness/missing fields or elements. etc. – keep moving until you get the result that you want or understand why you're not, and maybe you're going down the wrong path." Ultimately, the practitioner is responsible for dealing with data sets in the context of business demands – and this will likely entail understanding both what the <u>answer</u> should look like and what the <u>data</u> should look like.

Best practice advice

The key objective of V2V – and all of the communities managed by InsightaaS – is identification of best practices that can be used to advance the use of technology to drive better business outcomes. Asked to provide their input on best practices in applying the right data to the right question, group members focused on the following eight issues:

The right data is more of a journey than a snapshot

- Continuous improvement of data quality is very important (especially in smaller organizations, understanding how to continue to update both quantity and quality of data).
- Understand data provenance, and the transformations and operations done on data. Knowing the source and what's happened to data is key – some data scientists won't touch data without this info. Also, data sets created by joining data and bringing in data from other sources is another area to look at – it's not always an easy task to accomplish, and the resulting data needs to be reviewed before it is used.
- Success requires collaboration and implementation of a robust governance program – data dictionary, data lineage... – and having that information shared with the business

community, I think, is crucial to supporting a strong analytics department.

- There is real merit in defining data quality parameters – establishing a numerical measurement scale for data quality, so that you avoid subjective interpretations. Once we've got that, we can apply metrics, and if we can measure quality regularly, we stand a better chance of having better data – putting in a data quality firewall, if you will, with the right checks and balances to ensure that data is being entered into the system with acceptable quality in the first place. On top of that, look for ways of incorporating data quality into business functions and processes, so it's not an afterthought but actually an integral part of processes...shift towards 'doing it right' the first time.

Teamwork counts!
- Collaboration between business and IT is critical. I (as a practitioner) can gain access to any type of data that a business user might want – but I'm not necessarily going to know whether that's the data that the business user requires.

Don't forget the 'science' part of data science
- This is where 'real statistics' comes into play. When you're looking at statistics around your data and your analysis, and you see (for example) a low P-stat value, then you know that there's probably going to be a good relationship between two variables...you have to go back to some of those basics.

Don't overstate the certainty associated with a statistical inference
- One of the things that I see/have seen is that people are excited by the potential that data offers, and they have a tendency to draw conclusions that maybe they shouldn't. It's

a number – so (it's assumed that) numbers tell the truth, so if you use a number, then you're telling the truth. I see that in marketing…and I'm sure it permeates elsewhere. What I would really stress is, if you don't really understand what the numbers mean, consult with your experts, and make sure that the way that you're using the information is responsible.

Be cautious of systems that make repeated use of a single data set

- These kinds of questions get into play with AI and cognitive analytics. When you're building a system that's going to make decisions for you without supervision, you have to make sure that what you're implementing is a close to perfect as possible. But – no model is perfect. So you have to ask, how good is this model, and how long is it going to be good for us? How good is the data, and how long is it going to be good for us? When do we need to make a change?

Don't focus solely on the task at hand

- Data should be positioned as a strategic enabler, illustrating opportunities to create a new business or a new product offering. Many organizations are just focused on the issues/problems at hand from a tactical perspective. There is a need to take a more strategic view.
- Analytics initiatives deliver current outcomes from a business perspective, but also should be looking at answers that can't be found in what exists in the systems (except from connotations).
- Strategy vs. tactics – each requires different data. Strategic data is going to be different than tactical data – so is what you infer from either data set.

Prioritization matters

- Look strategically – best practice should be aligned with company strategy/direction. We can lose a lot of time sifting through data or answering questions that we don't need to answer – issues that are not necessarily relevant...
- Be cautious of requests for "vanity metrics" – data points that look good but which do not have much impact on decisions – vs. data that is actionable.

There is a need to iterate

- If your analysis seems clear, if you've identified a business problem and the analysis provides you with what you feel are the correct insights to move forward and you're confident, with the stats backing you up, then you're good to go. But if you hit a problem – for example, trying to relate two variables that shouldn't be related, then you have to be realistic – stop, and try to figure out what's going on. You need to understand what you're trying to accomplish, and whether you've accomplished it.
- When you first get the business question and the supporting data set – your client isn't asking whether you want a good or bad data set – it's usually the best possible and the only data set they have (and they always believe that it's good). After the first iteration, the first attempts to come up with and test a hypothesis, you have a pretty good idea of what the recommendations should be, what kind of changes would be desirable in data policies. Whether it's possible to implement these changes may be a different question...

Final thoughts: applying metrics

At the end of the conversation, the group was asked if there were any metrics or milestones that could be added to the best practice guidance. The consensus regarding metrics was clear:

- There's no 'one size fits all' set of metrics that can be applied to all problem solving analytics initiatives. In some cases, metrics focus on outcomes (ROI, reach, click-throughs, etc.); in others, the metrics focus on the data (timeliness, accuracy/precision, completeness). The right metrics are determined by both the business question and the evidence needed to address the question.
- That said, metrics should be designed to "minimize the risk of answering the *wrong* question" – for example, they should be selected to reduce tendency towards confirmation bias.
- Regardless of what metrics are selected, they should be specified in advance of the initiative. The metrics themselves will likely change from initiative to initiative – but "up front is more important than a specific number."

Chapter 3.

Monetizing Data: Identifying and Capturing the ROI on Analytics

Contributing community experts: Mary Allen, InsightaaS; Howard Bishansky, CenturyLink; Caterina Didio-Duggan, Information Builders; Prasanna Gunasekara, SmartProz; Francis Jeanson, I AM OPEN; Victor Magdic, Concept Flow; Jamie McDougall, Gore Mutual; Dean McKeown, Queen's School of Business; Jan Naranowicz, Rogers; Kelly Piggott, Information Builders; Michael Proulx, Pride Conflict Management; Paromita Ray; Dana Saltern, BusinessOne; Don Sheppard, ConCon Management Services; Vlad Skorokhod, eclairesys; Suresh Subramanian, Social Planning Council of Peel; Marie-Louise Thurton

Initial publication date: June 2018

Monetizing Data: Identifying and Capturing the ROI on Analytics

Identifying the sources of data value

The first stage in developing a perspective on monetizing data is to understand sources of data value: the areas that organizations focus on to identify return on analytics investments. Working group members were free to take any tack on the question that they believed would be fruitful, and were also asked to consider four possible value sources:

- Use of data to inform corporate/strategic decisions (e.g., allocating corporate resources to new activities identified through analytics)
- Use of data to inform immediate/direct/tactical actions (e.g., adjusting sales and marketing approaches to respond to preferences)
- Use of data to improve processes, control costs, drive efficiency/productivity, etc.
- Direct data monetization – sale of data or data-enabled products to generate revenue

The group discussions explored examples in each category, drawing on both private sector experiences, where 'monetization' can be measured directly in financial terms, and public sector contexts where monetization may take other forms. One group member observed that the four categories "are actually aligned – like a flow chart." After further discussion, the group identified an approach positioning the first three sources on a matrix defined by time to benefit and potential scope of return, setting the fourth source – direct data monetization – apart in its own category.

Figure 3-1. Sources of data value

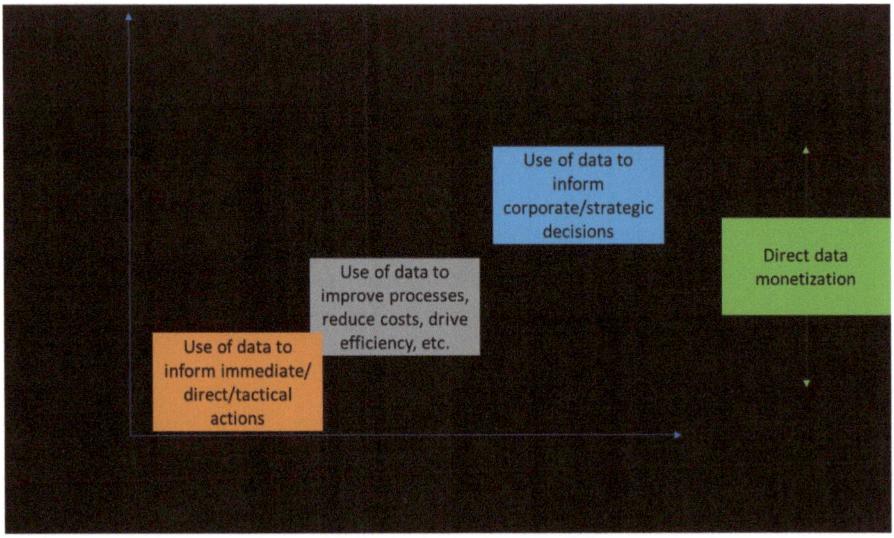

Use of data to inform corporate/strategic decisions

Direct data monetization

Use of data to improve processes, reduce costs, drive efficiency, etc.

Use of data to inform immediate/ direct/tactical actions

Use of data to inform immediate/direct/tactical actions

The category with the most immediate payback potential is use of data to inform tactical actions. The working groups offered multiple examples of monetizing data through immediate/direct/tactical actions, several of which involved d*ynamic pricing.* Often, this phrase is illustrated by the notion of soft drink machines that could raise or lower prices depending on weather conditions. There are other examples that help expand the concept. One cited by a working group member was Wasteless, which changes shelf pricing to help drive sales of products approaching their best-by dates; contributors pointed out that other firms, including Uber, employ similar approaches. Another was use of credit risk data to adjust financial services product rates, or even input from social media (such as pictures of dangerous hobbies posted to Facebook) used to determine insurance risk assessments.

One group member pointed to *systems of record*, such as ERP systems, as a potential input to direct/tactical decisions. A CRM system, for example, could recommend discounts for priority customers; an inventory system might increase or reduce sales incentives associated with products that are overstocked or in short supply; an accounts receivable system might highlight the need for extended credit or collection actions.

In each of these cases, there is a direct (and short) line from data/analytics to actions and results. The actions may not individually drive enormous returns, but ROI on these activities should be rapid and relatively easy to calculate, helping analytics professionals to demonstrate 'quick wins.'

Use of data to improve processes, control costs, and/or drive efficiency and productivity

The use of data to streamline processes provides the most intuitive set of data monetization examples, as many organizations' data strategies are driven by the need to cut costs or improve efficiency.

One good example of a direct link between data and value through improved processes is the use of sensor data to drive predictive maintenance. This can be monetized in several ways: by providing the insights needed to deliver managed services, where information helps to create a reasonable expectation of value for both buyers and sellers; by supporting the packaging of physical assets 'as-a-Service,' allowing suppliers to charge buyers for outcomes rather than assets (as in the famous case of aircraft engines that are billed on a usage basis, rather than sold as physical equipment); and/or through use of detailed operational insight, such as that gained from IoT, to reduce equipment or plant/facility downtime, thereby improving returns on costly assets.

Another example offered by the working group – one which was predicated more on reporting than advanced analysis – was a financial institution's creation of a self-service information portal. With the portal, the FI was able to streamline access to information, increasing customer satisfaction while reducing the cost and time associated with delivery of information to the client. This system is inherently scalable – addition of new clients does not require a great deal of time or have a major impact on system performance – and it has become a source of differentiation for the FI.

Other examples – illustrating both public and private sector scenarios – that were offered by working group members included:

- Analyzing sales data to identify upsell/cross-sell opportunities and embedding these insights into call centre scripts
- Using fuel consumption data to optimize transit or transport routes, and aligning transit routes with demand

- Workflow optimization achieved by identifying process bottlenecks and either adding resources at these points or defining more efficient pathways
- Standardizing on best/most efficient processes, improving throughput and reducing error rates
- Reducing school dropout rates by correlating data (such as test results and frequency) with student success.

- Achieving better utilization rates and citizen satisfaction by applying analytics to enforcement activities (property standards, parking, etc.), enabling staff to more efficiently identify and respond to requirements
- Using rich data sets to assign the right resource at the right time to respond to a call (which could apply to public safety or to private sector requests)
- Using marketing data to identify priority accounts and to determine the best course of action with each account
- Achieving better clarity or efficiency in core operations – for example, more accurately assessing the risk associated with a particular insurance policy or with a customer's insurance portfolio, or more quickly processing a claim
- Using a combination of video input indicating customer mood (happy, angry, anxious) with expert systems to help tellers or other customer service clerks to identify the most effective approach to the interaction

It should be noted that in several cases, the insights that lead directly to efficiency or cost reduction objectives provide additional benefits as well. For example, insight into likely component failure is essential to predictive maintenance, but it can also be used as input to purchasing (to prioritize suppliers of more reliable gear) or as an input to vendor management (requiring suppliers to address problematic components or systems). Data used to optimize transit schedules can also provide information that is important to transit system users, such as delay notifications.

And in some cases, the information and its use may create issues elsewhere in the business: for example, a system that identifies low-risk insurance clients who can be offered better rates will also identify high risk customers who need to be charged higher rates, meaning that someone within the business will need to establish adjusted prices and inform this latter group of increases.

Figure 3-1 positions initiatives that use data to improve processes, increase efficiency and/or reduce cost as having longer time-to-benefit and higher potential returns than using data to directly inform immediate/direct/tactical actions. The lengthier payback period is due to the requirement to translate insight into process change: there are additional steps between understanding the need for change and taking action that delivers target benefits. However, the potential magnitude of return on data-driven process change is greater as well, since processes can scale to address many different interactions, and can be refined over time to produce additional benefits.

Use of data to inform corporate/strategic decisions

As Figure 3-1 indicates, the use of data to inform strategic decisions is different from tactical uses and objectives in both payback period and the potential return on information. As the timeline implies (and as Figure 3-2 outlines), corporate strategy can't be quickly reflected in new, discrete processes; it moves organically through the organization, driving operational objectives, which in turn require staff to undertake gap analyses, followed by identification of alternatives/solutions and then, deployment of systems or processes that support operational and strategic objectives.

Figure 3-2. The path from strategy to solution

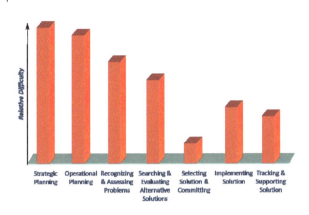

This view of corporate solution adoption, developed by Canadian IT industry executive Patrick Wade, posits that corporate decisions follow a pattern:

- Strategic planning – 'what are we going to do?'
- Operational planning – 'how are we going to do it?'
- Problem identification – 'what are the impediments to action?'
- Alternative/solution evaluation – 'what is the best way to address these impediments?'
- Solution selection and implementation – 'we are committed to a specific approach'
- Tracking and supporting the solution – 'we will optimize the capabilities that we have put in place to address known gaps that impact our operational ability to meet strategic objectives'

Source: Patrick Waid/Pinacon

If the path connecting data and strategy is long, though, the benefits gained from monetizing data by incorporating insights into corporate/strategic decisions can be compelling. Examples offered by the working group included:

- One business took a careful look at internal data on sales of bundles or related products and services, and found that it would be possible to migrate from a transactional to a subscription sales model. The company was able to increase revenues, improve cash flow and financial forecasting, and also provide better service to its customers – essentially reinventing itself and emerging as a larger, more profitable and more preferred supplier in its market.
- Looking to reduce warranty-related costs, Ford created a portal that demonstrated warranty repair rates for its dealers, and exposed that data to its dealer network. By linking this insight with a requirement for greater

accountability, Ford was able to reduce warranty-related expenses by 40%.

- General Motors used location information from its OnStar At Your Service to forge partnerships with firms like Priceline (hotel bookings), RetailMeNot (coupons), Entertainment Book (restaurant bookings) Audibooks.com and Dunkin' Donuts, connecting travellers with nearby options. This initiative both delivers new revenue streams to GM and makes its vehicles more attractive to car buyers; GM claimed to sell seven times more 4G-equipped vehicles in 2015 than the rest of the automobile industry combined.

- Public sector organizations have used data aggregated from their various internal systems and from external sources (e.g., social media) to gauge public interest in new or enhanced service offerings, and are able to use those same resources to disseminate information on the new services and to evaluate take-up, guiding future investment decisions.

- One group member cited an example where a financial institution aggregated data from across siloed business units to create a customer-centric business approach designed to generate improved business volumes and engagement/loyalty levels by clustering all relevant services around the customer's individual profile, rather than approaching customers who fit a particular segment profile with discrete product/service offers. This allowed the FI to build broader and deeper relationships based on communications reflecting the individual circumstances of the customer.

It's clear from the above that organizations using data to inform corporate/strategic decisions can obtain dramatic returns on information. It's important to remember, though, that these returns will take longer to materialize than benefits captured through use of data to inform tactical actions or data used to improve processes, drive efficiency or reduce cost. The total payback on monetizing data via improved strategy can be large, but the path can be long and uncertain; managers who are responsible for data-centric strategic initiatives are advised to develop plans that include milestone objectives and related controls, and to use relatively long timeframes for ROI/IRR/similar calculations.

Direct data monetization

In many cases, the phrase "data monetization" brings to mind a vision of firms that sell 'exhaust data' from their systems to third parties with congruent interests, but this is not yet (and may never be) a dominant mode of extracting value from data.

In Figure 3-1, direct data monetization is set apart from the other options covered in this section, and is shown as having a wide range of potential payback outcomes. There are certainly examples of firms that aggregate data to create discrete products (one group member noted Equifax in this context), firms that monetize data that

results from ongoing operations (such as Google and Facebook), and firms that build services based on available Big Data sets (an approach infamously exemplified by Cambridge Analytica).

These illustrations may not resonate with many existing organizations, but the working groups highlighted other examples that provide guidance to firms looking to sell (or buy) data. Group members cited industry-specific suppliers – for example, in health care and in marketing – who provide data sets that supplement internal resources, extending the base of clinical evidence used in diagnostic research or the scope of targeted communications supporting the introduction of a new product.

The clinical data example is illustrative of the opportunity and challenges associated with direct sales of data sets. In healthcare, a key objective – and source of value – is characterization of a population. This often requires the practitioner to expand core data sets by acquiring complementary data (e.g., from international laboratories) to expand the evidence base, increasing the number of records and/or the scope of the data. This observation illuminates two different potential sources of data value: suppliers of supplemental data obtain direct monetization through sales, and the practitioner's data set becomes more valuable (in terms of offering greater insight into pathologies and/or potential cures) by becoming more comprehensive. Broadly speaking, the same observations can be assigned to marketing data sources – additional contact with target customers (via lists, online display ads, etc.) is of value, and will attract investment by firms providing products or services, while in turn boosting revenue expectations for the buyers.

The key constraint here, and in similar instances, is the granularity of the metadata: 'joins' are only possible when different data sources can be matched according to key criteria. In marketing, this may be a fairly simple list – for example, key titles in specific departments working for firms in a target industry. In healthcare, requirements may be more complex, including some combination of age, gender, location, timeframes, existing pathologies and treatment regimens, and/or other factors. Other industries may have their own set of requirements. In all cases, suppliers and consumers of data need to come together on key metadata points and how they are measured and captured.

Observationally, it's interesting to note that there were relatively fewer observations in the direct data monetization category than in the other three areas – indicating, perhaps, that most firms looking for data monetization should focus on use of data to inform strategic or tactical decisions, or on using data to improve processes, control costs or drive efficiency or productivity, rather than direct sale of data sets. It's also interesting to observe that none of the examples given focused on direct sales of exhaust data (for example, sales of transaction data from a bridal gown shop to a specialty wedding cake baker) indicating that the sale of data as an adjunct to other business activities, while conceivable, isn't yet a common practice.

Data monetization best practices

Both working group calls delved into best practices associated with data monetization, with all 17 contributing professionals nominating practices that are important to capturing ROI from analytics.

A review of these nominations finds that they fall broadly into three categories. Some could be considered *foundational* – issues that are important to the practice of analytics as a whole, and not really specific to monetization. At the other end of the spectrum, some could be classified as *objective- or outcome-oriented* – suggestions that are important to identifying and capturing returns on data and analytics. And between these layers, as Figure 3-3 demonstrates, are a set of activities and objectives – *organizational, practice oriented* or concerned with *policy and compliance* – that connect foundational activities with the higher order objective/outcome-oriented practices.

Figure 3-3. Key issues in the data monetization 'pyramid'

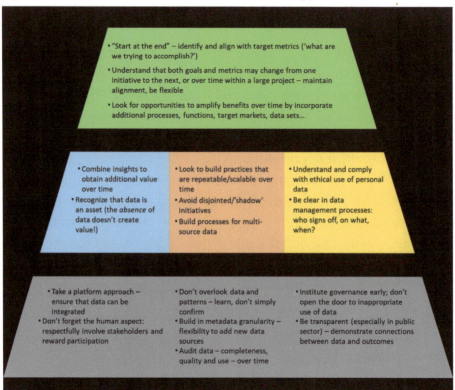

The arrangement of the guidance in Figure 3-3 serves a defined purpose. The recommendation here is that:

- Firms looking to monetize data should **begin by ensuring that they have covered off the foundational issues in the creation of their analytics disciplines**: they should have taken a platform approach that emphasizes integration, they should have a commitment to learning rather than confirmation, they should have a defined governance structure that protects the organization and its data, they should have an approach that addresses the need for broad participation in analytics initiatives, they should have sound metadata schemas, they should have a process that includes regular audits of data, and they should, to the extent that it is feasible, be transparent with respect to data sources, uses and outcomes.

- With the foundation layer in place, organizations focused on data monetization should **focus next on objective/outcome-oriented practices**. This begins by "starting at the end" – answering the business question 'what are we trying to accomplish?' and establishing success metrics. It includes a process definition that contains milestone objectives and which (especially for longer-term strategic projects) incorporates the flexibility to refine targets and metrics in response to evolving priorities or new opportunities. And this 'top of the pyramid' thinking should also explicitly include optimization reviews that provide stakeholders with a chance to explore ways of building on successful initiatives, amplifying benefits by applying now-proven proven methods to new/additional business requirements.

- The categories shown in the centre layer of the pyramid **connect monetization initiatives with fundamental capabilities by emphasizing organizational, practice-oriented, and policy and compliance activities.** The organizational guidance looks to translate platform capabilities and stakeholder engagement into a flexible project management approach and into opportunities for amplifying benefits attained through successful initiatives. The practice-oriented guidance is intended to alert management to potential pitfalls that can negatively affect data monetization. And the policy and compliance items are also intended to provide protection against gaps in governance. These might well not be a product of ill-intent – for example, an enthusiastic employee might see an opportunity to use a data set to achieve a desired outcome without recognizing that their proposed usage would be contrary to privacy policies or regulation – but regardless of motivation, there's a need to ensure that monetization objectives are pursued in a manner that is consistent with best corporate practices.

Data monetization: a process view

While the pyramid diagram provides a useful perspective on best practices in data monetization, the guidance produced by the working groups can also be arranged in terms of a process cycle. Figure 3-4 illustrates this approach.

Figure 3-4. Data monetization process cycle

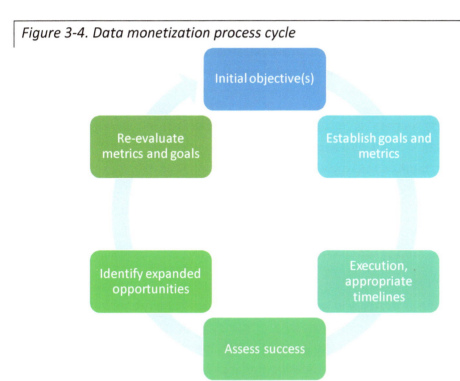

V2V/InsightaaS, 2018

Here, the foundation is assumed, and the business starts by identifying the objectives that it is pursuing – answering the 'what are we trying to accomplish?' question. This translates into a set of discrete project goals, which are formalized with metrics that establish whether/when the goals have been met.

The next step, "execution and appropriate timelines," might vary quite widely, depending on the nature of the initiative. As Figure 3-1 showed, if the data monetization activity consists of using data to inform immediate, direct tactical actions, the timeframe is likely to be relatively short; if the initiative is designed to use data to improve processes, reduce costs and/or drive greater efficiency, the timeframe for execution and evaluation will likely be longer; if the objective is to use data to inform strategic corporate decisions, the execution and evaluation timeframe is likely to be measured in years rather than months.

"Assess success" is important to any practice. For initiatives focused on tactical input or use of data to improve processes, this assessment can take place at the end of a project, while in strategic or direct data monetization activities, which may lack a clearly-defined endpoint, the assessment will need to be scheduled at specific project milestones (such as 6-12 months after launch of a new capability) or calendar dates (such as the end of a fiscal year).

Regardless of when the assessment takes place, stakeholders should examine whether and how they can enhance data monetization by expanding the use of successful practices, processes or approaches in other areas. This is the point at which the project team should look at how 'lessons learned' in one area might be applied to other challenges in the organization.

Beyond this identification of expansion possibilities, analytics leaders need to periodically undertake a formal re-assessment of metrics and goals. Were initial targets achievable – and achieved? What more can and should be expected from processes that are in place and functioning well? What changes in the business or the market might prompt establishment of new goals for data monetization? The answers to these questions, as is shown in Figure 3-4, re-start the cycle by establishing a new set of initial objectives.

Metrics used to evaluate data monetization

Metrics are uniquely important in understanding monetization: understanding whether monetization has actually occurred, and the extent to which it is compelling, requires measurement.

The working groups identified more than a dozen metrics that they have used in different contexts to set targets for and gauge success of data monetization. These fall into four categories: financial, marketing, technical and industry-specific.

Financial metrics are used to provide a dollar-denominated calibration of data monetization. Financial managers and senior executives are likely to require a financial view of monetization success, which means that one or more financial metrics are likely to be important in setting goals and measuring achievement. Financial measures that working group members have used in data monetization initiatives include:

- Return on investment (ROI)
- Internal rate of return (IRR)
- Net present value (NPV)
- Risk-adjusted return on capital (or in some cases, return on invested capital, or ROIC)
- Shareholder value (particularly important when direct data monetization is at the core of a business's offerings)

Marketing metrics apply, self-evidently, to measures of marketing success – but as marketing itself is an important area for data monetization, these metrics are relatively common in monetization-oriented initiatives, demonstrating the value of data and analytics in improving marketing outcomes. The key metrics used here are traditional marketing measures:

- Leads generated
- Changes in cycle times (less time from lead to close) or conversion rates (proportion of leads that close)
- Net promoter score (propensity of clients to recommend you as a supplier)
- Customer retention (or reduction in customer churn)
- Total/lifetime customer value

Industry-specific metrics are used to evaluate data monetization in a specific context – measures that are uniquely important to a particular business sector. Some industry-specific measures that have been used by the working group members include:

- Reductions in leakage/pollutants (mining or water distribution)
- Funding attracted (public sector, not-for-profit organizations, blockchain ICOs)
- Dropout rates (education), graduation rates (education - see earlier example) or recidivism rates (corrections)
- Quality of healthcare (as measured by patient success and lower readmission rates) and cost of patient care (healthcare).

Clearly, these measures aren't standard across business contexts, but they do represent important success metrics for professionals in different fields, and should be considered when establishing data monetization metrics and goals; even where the metric itself isn't inherently financial, it can represent a key measure of success, and may well tie back to finances in some way.

Technical metrics – measures that focus on underlying technology rather than business outcomes – are a bit out scope for this document, but they can be important to helping management to understand the cost/value of solutions used to pursue monetization goals. Metrics used by working group members in this context include:

- User adoption rates (number of users who rely on data to make business decisions)
- Value of decisions vs. analytics infrastructure (including hardware, software, data if it is acquired from outside the organization, and management costs)

One working group member noted that there is no 'unified model' that can be applied to all data monetization initiatives. To the extent that establishing goals and assessing success is important – and as Figure 3-4 demonstrates, these are key steps in data monetization – it's essential to identify metrics (usually, a combination of metrics) that are appropriate to discrete initiatives and/or continuous improvement, and important to the stakeholders who will ultimately decide whether the organization has achieved data monetization.

Chapter 4.

Establishing Analytics Within the Organization

Contributing community experts: Mary Allen, InsightaaS; Howard Bishansky, CenturyLink; Caterina Didio-Duggan, Information Builders; Ashraf Ghonaim, City of Toronto; Prasanna Gunasekera, SmartProz; Lewis Luo, ANI Networks; Victor Magdic, Concept Flow; Kartik Mathur, Scotiabank; Dean McKeown, Queen's School of Business; Hania Metulynsky, Ukrainian Credit Union; Jan Naranowicz, Rogers; Alice Rueda, Ryerson University; Dana Saltern, BusinessOne; Vlad Skorokhod, eclairesys; Suresh Subramaniam, Social Planning Council of Peel; Shrikant Subramanian, Accenture; Ken Tucker, Connaught Ealing; Igor Zaks, TenzorAI

Initial publication date: November 2018

Establishing Analytics Within the Organization

Factors in establishing demand for analytics within the organization

The first issue addressed in the V2V research concerned the conditions that are important to creating sustainable demand for analytics within the organization. What are the process, technical and cultural keys to creating optimal conditions for acceptance of analytics by staff, management and other business stakeholders?

The experts contributing to this report highlighted five primary issues that need to be addressed in the course of establishing analytics as an organizational force:

- Culture
- Demonstration of successes associated with early initiatives
- Process evolution
- Information utility
- Potential barriers to creating demand for analytics within an organization

Culture

One of the two working groups addressing the issue focused almost entirely on culture as the most important factor in establishing sustainable demand for analytics within the organization. A group member kicked off this discussion by observing that "analytics should really be 'bought not sold'" – that the prospects for success are greatest when demand is driven by staff and management requests for insight.

This would seem to argue against taking a top-down approach to mandating analytics adoption, but the working group was quick to identify the opportunity/need for executive champions to encourage analytics adoption. Rather than mandating use of a particular toolset, though, the advice from the working group was for executives to establish business performance metrics that require analysis of corporate data. The value of this approach is underscored if analytics practitioners highlight ways that data can be used to support strategy (and/or policy) development, providing management with facts that are helpful in establishing and communicating new business initiatives/directions to employees and other stakeholders. This presupposes that the organization has a commitment to evidence-based decision making; the working group believes that many organizations do use this approach today, and that more are coming to embrace it as the broader positive impact of fact-based decisions on business results is expounded in the business/professional press.

In addition to the corporate/strategic cultural impact of analytics, there is (as other working group members noted) also benefit to be gained in focusing at the department level. One member urged analytics practitioners to develop 'champions' within end-user departments to help develop acceptance of analytics at a functional level. If the analytics team can help staff members to "solve business problems with numbers" – to understand and capitalize on analytics – it develops allies who will in turn raise organizational awareness of the value that analytics can bring to the business.

It's worth noting that both the end-user departments and the analytics team learn from these types of interactions. As one working group member noted, "we often see people who are very good with analytical tools, but have no clue about the business domain – while on the other side, you have people who have massive experience in different domains, but have no clue about analytical tools." It's critical to develop communication that allows each group to learn from the other – else, the member stated, "you end up with people using irrelevant data to support irrelevant decisions."

Process evolution

One of the most important considerations in establishing any new resource within an organization is the ability to embed it within existing processes. Assets that become an intrinsic component of corporate activity are quickly woven into the business fabric; those that don't find a place within the workflow of an organization are often consigned to the dusty corners of the operation, considered to have potential value but little practical application.

For analytics to avoid this fate, the working group argued, practitioners need to look for ways to embed analytics within existing processes, and also, to establish processes that create an express link connecting analytics input with action and tangible value. One member emphasized that it is critical to create an approach in which "the time [from when] you get the raw data, all the way to when you deliver back high-level, evidence-based tangible results, is rapid." A clear, direct and documented process that begins with insight and ends with timely and effective change helps the entire organization to understand – and embrace – the impact of analytics.

Other working group members expanded on this theme. One noted that departments that may rely on lengthy processes to come to important decisions, such as HR and marketing, may be receptive to approaches that reduce the time needed to surface alternatives and identify the best go-forward options. Another noted that departments that use a set of key metrics to gauge current-state success, such as telesales, will react more positively to a process that results in quick but incremental 'wins' than to one that considers a wide range of conditions but requires a longer reporting timeframe.

Demonstrable success

A key to building cultural acceptance of analytics is to demonstrate its worth in a business context. One working group member noted that "what's important in creating sustainable demand for analytics…is back-to-basics success." The member observed that "people have to feel they're getting value [from analytics] – they have to see that they're better off because of it," adding that staff members "want to know whether analytics is going to make their job easier or whether it will provide more value, make more money for the company."

At a staff level, demonstrations of value can be informal: they can be delivered as a smoother workflow, as better feedback on processes and variations, as a means of demonstrating links between demands and responses, or in many other forms. Senior management, as one member noted, will likely require formal ROI analysis, to answer questions along the lines of "what is the value that we have seen" from investing in analytics capabilities? This member was quick to point out that oftentimes, a management decision to invest in analytics arises from "the realization that confusion is not the right way" to develop consensus and decisions, and that executives may themselves gain an understanding of the value of analytics once they begin using dashboards that support fact-based decision making. It is still important, though, for practitioners to capture the data needed to demonstrate the quantitative return that analytics delivers to the organization.

Information utility

The phrase "data democratization" has come into vogue over the past couple of years, describing environments where non-specialists have access to data that can be used to make decisions. In the context of this document, "Information utility" is intended to have a similar meaning. The important distinction between the two phrases is based on the idea that access doesn't necessarily result in better, fact-based decision making processes – and as a result, the emphasis here is on the impact rather than availability of data.

Several working group members cited information utility as a key factor in establishing sustainable demand for analytics within the organization. One emphasized that this is both an organizational and an individual issue: individuals need to believe that the information they are accessing is good and accurate, "making my life easier" and/or contributing to improved professional or corporate performance, while organizations need evidence that data is being accessed and used inside (and potentially outside) the business in order to justify ongoing/expanding investments in analytics.

Figure 4-1. Key factors in establishing demand for analytics within the organization

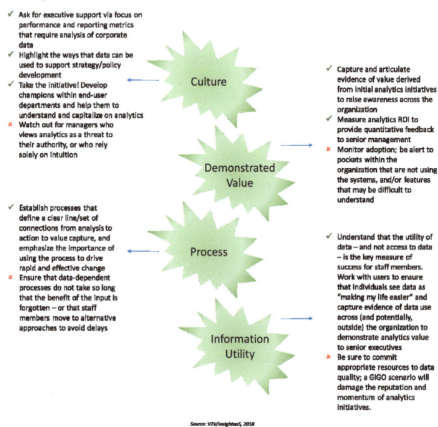

✓ Ask for executive support via focus on performance and reporting metrics that require analysis of corporate data
✓ Highlight the ways that data can be used to support strategy/policy development
✓ Take the initiative! Develop champions within end-user departments and help them to understand and capitalize on analytics
✗ Watch out for managers who views analytics as a threat to their authority, or who rely solely on intuition

Culture

✓ Capture and articulate evidence of value derived from initial analytics initiatives to raise awareness across the organization
✓ Measure analytics ROI to provide quantitative feedback to senior management
✗ Monitor adoption; be alert to pockets within the organization that are not using the systems, and/or features that may be difficult to understand

Demonstrated Value

✓ Establish processes that define a clear line/set of connections from analysis to action to value capture, and emphasize the importance of using the process to drive rapid and effective change
✗ Ensure that data-dependent processes do not take so long that the benefit of the input is forgotten – or that staff members move to alternative approaches to avoid delays

Process

✓ Understand that the utility of data – and not access to data – is the key measure of success for staff members. Work with users to ensure that individuals see data as "making my life easier" and capture evidence of data use across (and potentially, outside) the organization to demonstrate analytics value to senior executives
✗ Be sure to commit appropriate resources to data quality; a GIGO scenario will damage the reputation and momentum of analytics initiatives.

Information Utility

Source: V2V/InsightxxS, 2018

Cautions/potential barriers to creating demand for analytics within an organization

What 'gotchas' might inhibit successful introduction and expansion of analytics within a particular corporate environment? The responses offered by the working group mirror the factors cited as important considerations *for* the establishment of analytics within the organization:

- *Culture:* A common desire to obtain fact-based insight to decisions is not, as one member pointed out, the starting point in all organizations. The member stated that in an organization that he had experience with, "culture was a major roadblock" – not just to establishing analytics across the organization, but even as a standalone project. The push-back actually came from the senior leadership ranks, where executives took the position that they were the decision makers in the organization, asking "why would I hire a machine to do my job?"
- *Comfort:* At an individual level, employees may be uncomfortable with the tools that establish data as an input to action, and/or with the entire notion of predicating decisions or action on data rather than domain knowledge.
- *Expectations:* Several working group members emphasized the idea that data is a tool "to provide details," not a panacea that will address all possible issues. One likened analytics to self-driving cars, which "cannot tell you where to drive" or "what to do with your life" once you arrive at a destination.
- *Innovation:* Another observation of the working group is that to be successful, analytics practitioners need to ensure that a reliance on data does not become a block on innovation. Management looking to introduce a new strategy will "not have data directly relevant" to the untried approach; decision processes requiring historical data may block important novel ideas.
- *Relevance:* It seems self-evident that relevance should be demonstrated before new strategies are launched, but working group members cited examples of unrooted analytics initiatives driven from IT/practitioners and from business management. In the first case, analytics can be an

outgrowth of the observation that the corporation has potentially-beneficial data, and in the second, executives may get the idea that "everybody is doing it, we've got to do it too."

The extent to which these 'gotchas' exist within an organization, and the best methods of addressing them, will vary by context. They are highlighted here because one or more is likely to emerge during the process of establishing analytics within the organization, and practitioners should be attuned to these potential problem areas and aware of the need to develop responses if/as they arise. Tactics that were mentioned during the working group discussions included:

- Establish a "council:" If the key issue is *relevance*, or if objections centre on data accuracy and completeness, it may be possible to convene a "council" drawn from different areas of the organization – management, users, analytics practitioners, IT, and potentially individuals with deep knowledge of data availability and usage constraints – to highlight questions that can or can not be addressed with data, to understand issues in applying data to operational challenges, and to short-circuit avenues that are unlikely to deliver real benefit to the business.
- Build a "balanced score card:" A balanced scorecard, evaluating the application of data to specific objectives, can help address several of the 'gotchas' listed above. By demonstrating the ways that data contributes to success, as well as the requirements that are not met by data, practitioners can help manage expectations, increase comfort and close culture gaps.
- Establish processes that align data collection with new initiatives: where the concern is stifling *innovation*, one

possible approach is to create processes for capturing information that provides feedback on new directions, enabling the organization "to correct [its] trajectory and to react and to make appropriate changes."

The impetus for establishing analytics: top-down or department-out?

Broadly speaking, analytics can take one of two paths into corporate culture: it can gain momentum from success within a specific department or function, or its use can be mandated by senior management. The working group was asked to assess the advantages of both approaches – and while there are merits and challenges with both approaches, the importance of a visible senior leader is clear in all success scenarios.

Top-down

One member noted that "leadership comes from the top" – sometimes the CEO, sometimes the CIO, sometimes a department head, but it's never or almost never the case that "front-facing workers say 'we need to develop analytics within the organization'."

The majority of working group members reinforced the importance of senior management in the process of establishing analytics within the organization. This can be as simple as "thou shalt do the following," or it can take the form of mandating use of tools to produce dashboards and/or reports.

One extension of this top-down approach is for senior management to require information – for status updates and/or for compensation purposes – that will in turn require analytics as a means of satisfying the reporting requirement. This differs from a mandate to use tools, aligning analytics with outcomes rather simply relying on management fiat to drive adoption.

The caution associated with top-down approaches is the potential for users to not fully buy in to management's directives. As one member observed, "unless there is buy-in at the level of people who actual understand the context of the data, [analytics initiatives are] going to fail."

Department-out

In cases where analytics is established first within a department rather than as a result of a top-down mandate, demand is often driven by a need for rapid access to information. Even in environments that have basic dashboards, individual groups may need accelerated inputs – "quick decision-making points, instead of daily or weekly reports." With success comes awareness and expanding demand: "they're showing other departments the use cases and the value they're getting...then all of a sudden, it expands."

Department-out is important in many different contexts. In large/mature organizations, department-led initiatives can serve as prototypes that other functions (or a centre of excellence) can use as models elsewhere in the business. In (often, smaller) organizations that lack experience with using data to drive decisions and where senior management isn't pressing for analytics adoption, department-out initiatives may be the only way that analytics can take root within the business.

The best of both worlds?

So – is there a 'best answer' to the question posed at the top of this section? At least one group member believes that there is: "when it's top down the likelihood of success is much higher" – though the member added "when it's bottom-up [the practitioner] gets to work on more interesting projects." One alternative approach that captures some of the benefits of both approaches is establishment of a centre of excellence, which reflects senior management endorsement and has the flexibility to work with individual departments on projects aligned with context-specific needs.

Another observation is that industry and organizational maturity both matter to the prospects for success of analytics initiatives – especially for top-down approaches. The argument here is that while some firms and sectors have been slow to embrace data-driven business processes, many "now know that they need" analytics, which increases both the likelihood that senior management will mandate evidence-based approaches and the receptivity of staff to using data in decision making. This implies that over time, demand for analytics becomes more sustainable due to a higher level of staff and management knowledge/awareness of its importance and benefits.

In the end, it may be the case that both top-down and department-out momentum is required to build a viable context for analytics. As one working group member stated, "top-down is important – the buy-in, the executive sponsorship – but it's also extraordinarily important to get buy in from people who actually...have a vested interest" in using analytics to achieve tangible goals. Another member expanded on this point, noting that analytics is best driven "top-down when it comes to adoption, culture change, leadership and sponsorship, resources allocations and the planning. When it comes to the implementation and the execution, I would say bottom-up [is better] because the scope can be more manageable.

The ability to deliver tangible results on the ground are much higher and much faster as well."

Figure 4-2. Balancing top-down and department-out analytics adoption

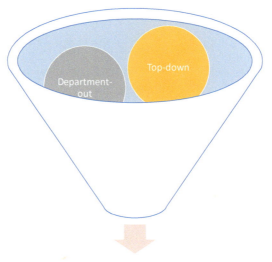

Multi-pronged approach capitalizes on
management, user and practitioner input

Source: V2V/InsightaaS, 2018

Key inputs to the process of establishing analytics within the organization

In many ways, the issues discussed to this point in this document cover issues that are important to building corporate receptivity to analytics: metaphorically, the actions needed to set the table for analytics success. A reasonable next question is, what groceries are needed for the menu – or in an analytics context, what inputs are needed for success? In some ways, this question served as a summary of the issues raised in the previous sections of this report:

working group members highlighted *skills and training, policies, data quality, relevance* and *solution licensing.*

Skills and training

One input that both working groups considered to be critical to success was *skills*. This includes the technical skills needed to analyze data, but one working group member specifically called out communications as a critical skill linking analytics potential and acceptance, and another highlighted skills related to developing and managing teams. A third member added that analytics groups need to include people who "love data – [who will act as a] data evangelist...interpret data, wrangle data, and who's able to work with" senior executives and internal client teams.

Another member branched into a discussion of training, particularly "training up your business people." The member noted that these are the staff members "who have the most knowledge about your products, your customers, new strategies and trajectories."

It's beneficial to teach these business professionals how to do some data analysis on their own. However, the member stressed that business users shouldn't "need to worry about getting into the math and the stats bit – instead, "they should have enough knowledge and skills to understand what is possible. How do we look at the data? How does it actually get analyzed? What kind of tools do we have? What things can we look for?" This, the member stated, is the piece of training that needs to be done for your business people. They know what's going on. They'll be the ones who can discover something new" – because from a business perspective, analytics "is not about pure math and pure data, it's also about instinct. It's about what you as a member of that company know, understand and feel." Additional commentary on this issue emphasized the need for business professional training to highlight not only the ways to use analytics but also the constraints on analytics: managers who can use tools but don't understand the correct application of a data set or model may mistake accidental or inappropriate outcomes for 'evidence' supporting a decision.

Commenting on this issue, a group member added that in the end-user community – and especially, within smaller organizations – "you'll have varying levels of skill, and not everyone will have the same disposition towards analytics…there is value in having cross-organizational training" on both tools and basic data concepts.

This is not, the member added, the basis for a complete solution in all companies: in some cases, outsourcing to suppliers who can develop intuitive self-serve systems tied to specific needs may be preferable to training as a way of quickly acquiring needed skills.

Policies

Policies are an essential component within the analytics toolkit. A top-down requirement for evidence-based management approaches is one area where policy has a direct impact on the prospects for analytics viability within the organization; if executives insist on data-driven decision processes, departmental staff will rely on analytics for input to communications with their managers.

Policies are also important to safeguarding the business against misuse of data. One working group member highlighted the importance of data management by noting the need for firms to be sure that the use of data to answer a question posed by a manager in marketing or sales doesn't compromise GDPR or other privacy regulations. Policies that mandate use of data as inputs to corporate metrics or decisions are discussed above, but they also bear mention here, as they, too, are important as inputs to analytics success.

Data quality

Like policies, the importance of data quality was touched upon in the first section of this report, but it also should be included in the list of attributes required for analytics viability within an organization. One working group member focused data quality comments on the need to establish a single version of the truth: if, for example, different departments measure revenue or cost in different ways, reports or dashboards that are inconsistent with 'known facts' will invite rejection not just of a specific data point or conclusion but of analytics as a means of building corporate understanding. A second member took up this theme, noting that "you don't want to start making decisions based on the wrong data," and highlighting the importance of good data quality as organizations move to self-service solutions: users who are willing to work with analytics tools need access to reliable inputs, as they are unlikely to be able to parse through data sets to identify anomalies buried in original sources.

Relevance

This point spans both the previous parts of this report and other attributes listed in this section. One working group member highlighted an example of a firm that drove enthusiastic acceptance and long-term demand for data by working closely with staffers in different business groups (drawing on communications and team management skills) to build a deep understanding of different roles and potential applications of analytics to core processes. The key, the member believed, is to "focus on the employee role and to make sure that the information that they are receiving is information that can help them in a concrete and practical way with their daily work." The member added that "if you're planning a program, spend time with front-line workers...make sure that they get something that's relevant to their role. Make sure that there isn't information overload because sometimes if you present people with a bunch of stuff that they can't use, then they go blank."

Another group member noted that the pursuit of relevance comes back to some of the skills issues noted above. "When you are implementing analytics, it's all about project management, understanding the user needs" – successful organizations have individuals who "understand the requirements from the [user] departments...and communicate that to the people who are developing the solution" – for example, within IT.

Solution licensing

One member pointed to a disconnect within his organization, where the tool used by the central analytics team wasn't licensed for use within the end-user departments. As a result, "we're able to produce reports to them that are very fast...[but] when we hand reports over. [users] have no ability to actually be able to manipulate the data, once they receive it. They rely on us to go back and adjust things." The member added that it's important to distribute both data *and* tools, so that "the audience that receives the results can kind of just go in and dig into the information itself."

Another participant took this discussion down a different path, identifying tool selection as a key step. With the wide range of solutions available (both direct from software vendors and packaged by integrators), companies can choose between platforms that support a wide range of requirements, point products that deliver rapid responses to a limited set of questions, or solutions that meet some combination of needs. Firms looking to adopt or expand analytics within their operations, the team member said, should develop (or engage firms that have developed) the ability to identify the solutions that best support the capacity for teams to collaborate as they identify and pursue group business goals. This point was made in a second working group session as well, with a member stating that "it's very, very important to be sure that the tools are relevant for the task" – otherwise, analytics can result in "outcomes that are not suitable for the business."

Figure 4-3. Critical success attributes needed to establish analytics within the organization

Skills and training
- Both technical skills and communications/teamwork
- Invest in training business professionals on analytics potential and limitations

Policies
- Management emphasis on evidence-based, data-driven decision processes
- Ensure that data access is managed in accordance with regulatory requirements

Data quality
- Especially important in supporting self-service

Relevance
- Focus on the employee role – information should tie to daily work in a concrete and practical way

Solution licensing
- Select and license tools to support teams as they pursue business goals

Source: V2V/InsightaaS, 2018

The evolution of analytics within the organization

In most environments, analytics adoption starts with an initial project (or series of limited-scope projects) and – where successful – expands to become an important capability within a function or department, and ultimately, a part of the corporate routine. In the working group meetings, participating experts were asked about this process: how does this path start and evolve? How does analytics success within a function spawn demand and success in other areas of the business? And, what can/should an analytics professional (or a senior business manager) do, to expand use of analytics?

Getting the ball rolling

The discussion on this topic started with the observation that organizations are likely to see the value of analytics "immediately, based on the insights that [new adopters] get on their organization." The key at this stage, the group member added, is to be sure that "everybody is seeing" the value that analytics brings to the company. This theme was expanded upon by other group members: one emphasized the importance of quick turnaround time on requests ("that builds confidence in the [analytics] department") and a focus on working with initial adopters to align scope with business needs as understanding of the business value of analytics expands.

Another member drew a distinction between environments where analytics is adopted in responses to management KPIs versus situations where analytics arrives as a means of helping staff members to address "a very particular problem" pertaining to "a very specific task." In the first scenario, adoption expands quickly, and the key task is to increase the depth of data use; in the second, expansion occurs "if you are seeing results that are being delivered in one [area of the business] and they are not delivered in another –

and if analytics is viewed as one of the key drivers...then you get pressure," from senior management or simply as a result of internal competitiveness, for adoption of analytics in other areas. As the conditional statements above note, this is far from a certain path to broad analytics adoption: in fact, another working group member has found that in "larger organizations where departments don't really talk to each other...there are more roadblocks [to expanding analytics demand] than we actually tend to believe."

Timing

Despite the consensus regarding the importance of rapid turnaround of initial requests, and fast time-to-benefit for early analytics initiatives, the initial stage of proving the value of analytics is likely to take years, not months; one working group member described an environment where "once you start showing results and use for the departments, you can see them coming left, right and center asking for different things, expanding it, matching that data with other information," but adding that "it took about two years" to get to the point where analytics had become a core element of the business's culture. There can be several reasons for the length of the initial adoption stage: some that were cited by the working group include greater than anticipated complexity of first issues (and as a result, the analytics needed to address them); unanticipated gaps in data quality, and problems expanding scope from an initial proof of concept to a production-level initiative.

Integrating analytics within broader corporate policy structures

In many cases, finding new capabilities integrated within core practices is the best proof of corporate commitment to an IT/business initiative. With this in mind, working group members were asked to provide examples of how analytics has been integrated into an organization's policy framework.

This is a difficult question, as it looks past discrete projects to a state where analytics is embedded within the organization's DNA. As one working group member said, "I always struggle a bit with this kind of question." One the one hand, we "think of analytics projects…they're solving [a specific] problem that the company has." When analytics is positioned as a core element of strategy and policy, "guiding principles come into play – there are certain things we will do to solve a problem, and there are certain things we will not do." Analytics is not, at this point, simply a tool used to address a problem – it's an organizational practice that needs to be subject to the same operational, ethical and privacy strictures that are applied to any business process or capability.

The discussion on how to achieve this in an organization that has evolved to the point where analytics is an intrinsic element of corporate policy led to a number of different observations. One member provided a clear (and fascinating) operational template. In his opinion, large organizations are moving towards having the centre of excellence for analytics and decision science and the enterprise data office report to a single leadership position or team, so that they have "common goals – the data office…is integrating [the data strategy] into the DNA of the organization's business strategy'"

At a functional level, the operational template could include a data office with responsibility for a multi-tenant data lake that acts as a central resource – "maybe Project A is bringing a data feed and Project B is going to use that data feed" as the basis for a model." Three parties govern data use: a data steward, who represents the interests and responsibilities of the business users, a data custodian, who is responsible for data ownership from an IT perspective, and the privacy office. These three stakeholder groups enter into a "data sharing agreement. It is a contractual agreement…an artifact which brings the business perspective and IT buy-in, as well as the privacy office buy-in. All three parties have to sit at the table and agree" on issues like "who will bring the data, who will share the data, what are the data sources, are they mature enough, who are the users of the data." The working group broadly endorsed this approach, adding that it would support a wide range of innovative projects, and support development of "the culture of analytics within the organization."

Figure 4-4. From project to practice: the evolution of analytics within the organization

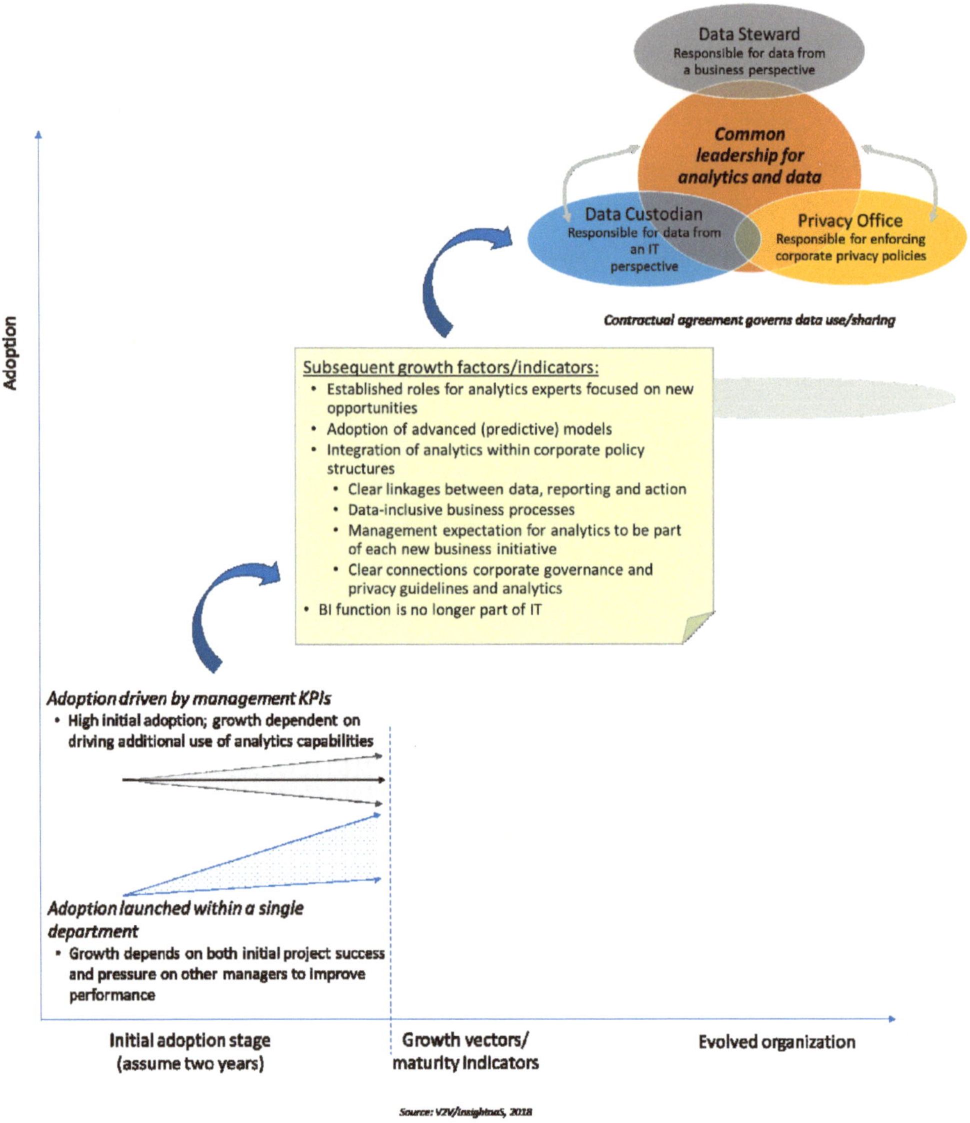

Data Steward
Responsible for data from a business perspective

Common leadership for analytics and data

Data Custodian
Responsible for data from an IT perspective

Privacy Office
Responsible for enforcing corporate privacy policies

Contractual agreement governs data use/sharing

Subsequent growth factors/indicators:
- Established roles for analytics experts focused on new opportunities
- Adoption of advanced (predictive) models
- Integration of analytics within corporate policy structures
  - Clear linkages between data, reporting and action
  - Data-inclusive business processes
  - Management expectation for analytics to be part of each new business initiative
  - Clear connections corporate governance and privacy guidelines and analytics
- BI function is no longer part of IT

Adoption driven by management KPIs
- High initial adoption; growth dependent on driving additional use of analytics capabilities

Adoption launched within a single department
- Growth depends on both initial project success and pressure on other managers to improve performance

Adoption

| Initial adoption stage (assume two years) | Growth vectors/ maturity indicators | Evolved organization |

Source: V2V/insightoS, 2018

The path forward

At the conclusion of both working group sessions, members were asked to identify important future steps in analytics, leading to the state where BI, analytics and AI are common components of business operations. This was not intended as a comprehensive exploration of this topic (which could easily fill several additional reports!), but rather, as a means of identifying signposts on the journey to establishing analytics within the organization.

The working groups began by putting the question in context, noting that over time – within the initial stage identified in Figure 4-4, and beyond it – there is a need to move systematically from initial BI deployment towards increased capabilities. One important step is the development of what a member referred to as "the data stewardship role" – meaning here, a staff function whose job it is to "create reports, present findings and look at alternative ways" of using data to drive business decisions.

Another vector raised by the group is adoption of predictive models, giving management "a chance to think of where they want to take their company in the future." This should develop incrementally, one group member argued, building on core BI platforms to develop analytics-based and machine algorithms that bring AI capabilities without "disruptive changes."

One way that this may come about, particularly within smaller organizations, is in the form of embedded expert systems. One working group member who works with SMB clients said that for the firms he's engaged with, "having that type of [advanced analytics/AI] talent in-house is unlikely...what I'm seeing is a refinement of the tools we have...there's still a lot of maturity that can be developed in terms of allowing people who aren't data-focused as part of their day-to-day jobs to be able to derive value" from advanced analytics.

In larger organizations, there are likely to be multiple paths forward for analytics capabilities. At one level, specialists will deploy analytics/AI-based systems that provide superior performance in discrete functions (such as fraud analysis). At another level, it seems likely that analytics will move from being a stand-alone competency to a capability that exists within many different parts of the operation, as "double-deep" employees make analytics part of their function.

These larger organizations will also lead the way in organizational innovation that unlocks enterprise-wide data potential. This starts with the establishment of the Chief Data Officer (CDO) role: a senior leadership team member who champions a data/analytics culture, responsible for managing data as a corporate asset. The working group believed that the CDO will act as "the driving force behind defining, designing, and executing the [corporate] data strategy and overcoming any roadblocks in its execution life cycle [as well as] shifting the focus of analytics from being an enabler" to positioning analytics as a key component of daily business activity. The expansion of the organization continues to broader integration of the Data Scientist, Data Analyst and Data Engineer roles, providing the capacity to build advanced models, provide relevant analysis and enable self-serve systems that expand the reach of data within the organization.

Cautions

While the path forward for analytics is bright, it is not without potential potholes. A group member pointed out that there is a tendency to use analytics to develop KPI-managed operations, but that unless the KPIs are well designed, behaviour will not map to desired outcomes: "people do what management inspects, not what management expects." The member added that strategic alignment between tools, models, KPIs and objectives is critical – "if the alignment is good, [analytics] is extraordinarily helpful" to establishing sound corporate management practices.

Another group member highlighted the difficulty of expanding analytics and AI in a practical context. "The dollar sign is going to be the ultimate metric...by adopting tools, you are driving revenue or profit," but in the reality of environments with limited resources and multiple competing interests, analytics will be constrained as much by the realities of corporate politics as by the cost/benefit associated with its use. This is especially true with AI, the member believed: "analytics supports decision-making – but decision makers have to decide whether to adopt analytics," and may view AI as a threat to their positions.

Outlook

Despite the pitfalls noted above, the group felt comfortable positioning increased use of analytics and AI as a logical destination on the long-term roadmap. One member observed that "in the bigger picture, [analytics adoption] is moving ahead very quickly – much quicker than a lot of people though was possible. A lot of that is driven at the top, by boards saying "hey, we've got to get in on this, if we don't, we're going to lose out. And the business successes are quite clear as well." Other members noted that with respect to AI, the trend may be ahead of real business use cases – but that overall, analytics is becoming an increasingly-important component of corporate management practice.

Near the end of one of the working group sessions, a member provided a concise summary explaining the outlook for increased use of analytics, saying "the more time progresses, we have more demand for services, and internal resources [are not keeping pace] - the imbalance between supply and demand [and pressures arising from industry trends towards 'smart' solutions] make it inevitable that we will proceed with AI and start to rely more and more on machines. You have to find a way to make the limited supply that you have meet the increased demand" – and analytics will play a key role in helping to maintain this balance.

Contributing Experts

Acknowledging the subject matter experts whose insight and guidance have shaped the contents of this book

Contributors to this document

Mary Allen
Chief Content Officer, InsightaaS

Co-founder of InsightaaS, Mary has devoted two decades to understanding and communicating key trends shaping Canadian and global IT markets. She has authored hundreds of reports, articles and analyses on advanced technologies.

Caterina Didio-Duggan
Area Marketing Director, Information Builders

Caterina is an experienced B2B marketing who creatively uses multiple channels of marketing - email, direct mail, social media, events, promotions - to deliver a compelling message to drive executable leads and results.

Dean McKeown
Associate Director, Master of Management Analytics, Queen's University

Dean has held many roles in the post-secondary education sector, and has served as a trustee on several non-for profit boards. Dean's research interests include big data analytics, governance, privacy and public policy.

Francis Jeanson
Data Science and AI entrepreneur

 Francis is the found of Datadex, a firm that builds AI-drive software services and solutions for collaboration and data science. He previously worked at the Ontario Brain Institute as Program Lead and Manager for Informatics and Analytics.

Michael Proulx
Founder, Pride Conflict Risk Management

 Michael is an enthusiastic and collaborative professional with proven experience in academic and corporate environments, well-versed in capital/ investment strategies, risk management assessment and analysis, client relationship management.

Victor Magdic
Managing Director, Concept Flow

 Victor holds a law degree from Osgoode Hall Law School and is trained in numerous IT methodologies and disciplines. He has a strong focus on the financial services industry, cloud and business blockchain.

Jan Naranowicz

Reporting Analyst and WFM Leader, Rogers Communications

Within Rogers, Jan has a leadership role for support of the Customer Activations, Migrations, and Onboarding departments. He is responsible for daily SLA targets for all departments, and for each department's capacity plan and monthly budget.

Vlad Skorokhod

Principal and Director of Data Science, eclairesys

Vlad has a Ph.D. engineering, M.Sc. in experimental physics, and is a co-inventor of 51 US patents. With a background in experimental science and system engineering, he now applies scientific principles and data science to complex business problems.

Dana Saltern

Director, BusinessOne Corporation

Dana is an executive advisor with 20+ years of transformation experience in both the public and private sectors, driving strategic initiatives by planning and implementing solutions to increase engagement, performance and innovation.

Don Sheppard
Emerging technology consultant, standards advisor, author/writer

Don has worked to help de-mystify ICT as an engineer, a manager, and a consultant for more than twenty-five years. He is best known for his involvement in ISO standards for open systems interconnection and for cloud computing.

Kelly Piggott
Marketing Analyst, Information Builders

Kelly is a marketing ninja with an eye for detail and an ear for ideas. She works with the Information Builders team to build their personal and professional brands, human-to-human. She holds a BSc in Computer Science and Logic from U of T.

Prasanna Gunasekara
Partner, SmartProz

Prasanna is a leader in business transformation through automation and innovation. He has recently formed SmartProz after 16 years with City of Brampton, leading a team that helped business leaders solve problems via process re-engineering.

Howard Bishansky
Director, Channels & Alliances, CenturyLink

 Howard manages relationships with Canadian business partners for CenturyLink. He has worked in a variety of analytics-related roles, and cites a thorough understanding of BI and information management and governance as key attributes.

Suresh Subramaniam
Data Scientist, Social Planning Council of Peel

 Suresh is an experienced senior management professional who is able to mine insights from large sets of structured, semi-structured or unstructured data, applying statistics, visualization and modeling to facilitate in-depth exploration.

Brian Joynt
Senior Vice-President, International, Information Builders

 Brian is the Senior Vice-President, International for Information Builders. Since joining IB in 1998, he has held a variety of Canadian and global sales management roles, and has led the company in its shift towards value-based pricing and selling models.

Kartik Mathur
Senior Portfolio Manager, Scotiabank

Kartik's strong understanding of the relationship between technology and strategic business interests enables him to lead teams that design innovative and pragmatic solutions that combine cloud computing and data science.

May Chang
Former EVP, Finance and Operations, Markham Stouffville Hospital

An inspiring and strategic leader with extensive experience in executive leadership roles for large multi-site hospitals, May has developed and led creative innovations that set the platform in healthcare sector.

Glenda Schmidt
EMBA candidate; former Senior Business Relationship Manager, OECM

Glenda works at understanding complex issues, capitalizing on connections, and collaborating with teams. She has professional experience in strategic and tactical planning, analytics, process development and other key business requirements.

Jeffrey Veffer
Senior Consultant, IoT and Analytics, Jones Lang LaSalle

Jeffrey manages IoT product delivery as well as business/partnership development at JLL. Prior to JLL, Jeffrey was Director, Internet of Things and Business Intelligence for Brookfield Global Integrated Solutions.

Jamie McDougall
Vice President, Business Intelligence & Analytics, Gore Mutual

An experienced business executive with a demonstrated history of delivering innovation and excellence, Jamie is skilled in the application of advanced analytics capabilities to enable management in property and casualty insurance.

Hania Metulynsky
Business Analyst, Ukrainian Credit Union

Hania has held multiple management roles in data and service companies. For the past eight years, she has been leading large data projects for Ukrainian Credit Union, an $800 million (assets) financial institution with over 125 employees.

Mitchell Ogilvie
Senior Solutions Architect, Information Builders

Mitchell specializes in the data integration, data quality and master data management space. He has deep experience in helping customers assess, scope and deliver enterprise information management solutions across different verticals.

Igor Zaks
President and CEO, TenzorAI

Igor has extensive experience working for and advising both major corporations and financial institutions in working capital, trade and supply chain financing, and in building highly-customized intelligent engines supporting credit, risk and pricing.

Ken Tucker
Independent Consultant, Connaught Ealing Solutions

Ken is focused on helping companies to leverage AI and analytics technologies in pursuit of corporate objectives. He has been involved in AI since the 1990s when he helped launch a predictive modeling solution for biomedical process control.

Michael Shin
Team Lead, Transformative Technology Adoption, Ontario Government

Michael is the Team Lead for a group in the Ontario Government that focuses on facilitating technology adoption by Ontario's small and medium sized businesses. He started his career as a management consultant with Deloitte and A.T. Kearney.

Alice Rueda
Ph.D. Candidate in Electrical Engineering, Ryerson University

Alice describes herself as a "data analytics enthusiast dedicated to provide seniors with dignified independent lifestyle through research, engineering, and educating the younger generation." She is a doctoral student in electrical engineering at Ryerson.

Lewis Luo
International Consultant, ANI Networking

Lewis is a researcher and advocate, working in public, private and academic environments to identify global solution opportunities that improve leadership, education and public policy.

Roman Zubarev
Partner, 29signals Consulting

An entrepreneur with experience in telco, IT consulting and automation, Roman has led several SMEs and large-scale IT projects. Currently a Master of Management Analytics candidate and an analytics consultant.

Pavan Jauhal
City of Toronto

Pavan is a Business Analyst for the City of Toronto. She has more than a decade of experience in IT, focused primarily on banking projects dealing with compliance and reporting. Making informed decisions from data analytics is my passion!

Ashraf Ghonaim
Strategic Management Consultant, City of Toronto

Ashraf has extensive experience in driving evidence-based strategic business change. His approach to business process performance improvement combines management methodologies with data mining, predictive modeling and scenario planning.

Shrikant Subramanian
Manager, Finance Transformation, Accenture

 Shrikant 's role spans Finance Transformation, Digital Product Management, IT Capabilities and Operations. He has worked on complex projects involving financial analysis and modeling with teams across Canada, USA, India and Argentina.

Paromita Ray
BI/Data Analyst, Total Credit Recovery Limited

 Paromita is a results-oriented BI analyst with experience within the public sector. She has worked with teams to develop requirements/specifications, align BI initiatives with business goals and report to non-technical stakeholders and senior executives.

Purushoth Ramu
Analytic Manager. LexisNexis

 Purushoth is the Analytics Manager for LexisNexis Canada, which provides research and information to legal professionals and law firms. He is enthusiastic and passionate towards the understanding the data and creation of data visualizations.

Contributors to V2V Meetups

In addition to publishing the research contained in this report, the V2V community has held a series of meetups that have helped to explore best practice positions with leading Canadian analytics professions.

A number of the co-creators listed above, including Dean McKeown, Michael Proulx, May Chang, Victor Magdic, Glenda Schmidt, Vlad Skorokhod, Kartik Mathur, Francis Jeanson, Jan Naranowicz, Hania Metulynsky and Prasanna Gunasekara – played an important role in vetting the V2V research positions with the broader community.

The live sessions also benefitted from the insights contributed by experts who joined the meetings to provide additional perspective. The V2V stakeholders would like to thank these thought leaders who contributed to the success of the live meetup events:

- Robert Eckersley, Director, Business Development, Information Builders
- Achille Ettorre, Faculty Member, International Institute for Analytics, and former Senior Director, Loblaws
- Sarah Sun, Chief Data Strategist, Goldspot
- Mukesh Sharma, Director, Data Qualify Management, Investment Division, Manulife
- Ganesh Iyer, Data Evangelist, Information Builders
- Joe Walsh, Senior PreSales System Engineer, Information Builders
- Michael Ray, Director, Data Management Branch, Ontario Ministry of Labour
- Yash Shrestha, former BI Consultant, Information Builders
- Kavita Khera, Senior Manager-Analytics, Ontario Ministry of Labour

Top row: Robert, Achille, Sarah; centre row: Mukesh, Ganesh; bottom row: Joe, Michael, Yash

Lead analyst

Michael O'Neil is Canada's leading IT industry analyst. Through the course of his career, he has he has helped executives at leading buy-side and sell-side organizations to capitalize on new technologies and accompanying business opportunities. O'Neil has authored hundreds of reports and whitepapers, and two acclaimed management books: *Building Cloud Value: A Guide to Best Practice, 2016* (with InsightaaS partner Mary Allen) and *The Death of Core Competency: A management guide to cloud computing and the zero-friction management future* (InsightaaS Press, 2014).

Founding member organizations

The V2V community was founded through a collaboration between Information Builders and InsightaaS.

About Information Builders

Information Builders provides the industry's most scalable software solutions for data management and analytics. We help organizations operationalize and monetize their data through insights that drive action. Our integrated platform for business intelligence (BI), analytics, data integration, and data quality, combined with our proven expertise, delivers value faster, with less risk. We believe data and analytics are the drivers of digital transformation, and we're on a mission to help our customers capitalize on new opportunities in the connected world. Information Builders is headquartered in New York, NY, with global offices, and remains one of the largest privately held companies in the industry.

Visit us at informationbuilders.com, follow us on Twitter at @infobldrs, like us on Facebook, and visit our LinkedIn page.

About InsightaaS

Dedicated to exploring "the 'why' in enterprise technology," InsightaaS was founded by Mary Allen and Michael O'Neil in 2013. The company operates Canada's deepest IT content website and provides strategic consulting and channel management guidance to leading firms in Canada, the US and abroad.

In 2015, InsightaaS launched the Toronto Cloud Business Coalition, a community dedicated to the co-creation of Best Practice guidance designed to accelerate adoption and use of cloud in Canada. The tremendous success of the group spawned many other professional communities and meetup groups – Vision to Value (V2V): The Economics of Data (community and meetup group), DC Foresight (community, meetup group and annual event), Transformative Technologies in Canada (community and meetup group), IoT Coalition Canada (community), the Canadian Analytics Business Coalition (community), and CIA-Plus (meetup group). These initiatives continue to help Canadian and global businesses to identify best practices in capturing value from advanced technology.

www.ingramcontent.com/pod-product-compliance
Lightning Source LLC
Chambersburg PA
CBHW041142050326
40689CB00001B/450